Elite • 179

Pike and Shot Tactics
1590–1660

KEITH ROBERTS

ILLUSTRATED BY ADAM HOOK
Consultant editor Martin Windrow

OSPREY PUBLISHING
Bloomsbury Publishing Plc

Kemp House, Chawley Park, Cumnor Hill, Oxford OX2 9PH, UK
29 Earlsfort Terrace, Dublin 2, Ireland
1385 Broadway, 5th Floor, New York, NY 10018, USA
Email: info@ospreypublishing.com
www.ospreypublishing.com

OSPREY is a trademark of Osprey Publishing Ltd

First published in Great Britain in 2010
Transferred to digital print in 2014

A catalogue record for this book is available from the British Library

Print ISBN: 978 1 84603 469 5
ePub: 978 1 78096 784 4
ePDF: 978 1 84908 266 2

Editorial by Martin Windrow
Design by Ken Vail Graphic Design, Cambridge, UK (kvgd.com)
Index by Alison Worthington
Originated by PPS Grasmere, Leeds, UK
Typeset in Sabon and Myriad Pro
Printed and bound in India by Replika Press Private Ltd.

MIX
Paper from
responsible sources
FSC® C016779

24 25 26 27 28   12 11 10 9 8 7

Acknowledgements
I would like to thank my friends for their support in my research over the years.
This is a large group, but i owe particular thanks to Richard Brzezinski, Neal Gray,
Dave Ryan and John Tincey.

Artist's note
Readers may care to note that the original paintings from which the colour plates
in this book were prepared are available for private sale. All reproduction copyright
whatsoever is retained by the Publishers. All enquiries should be addressed to:

Scorpio, 158 Mill Road, Hailsham, East Sussex BN27 2SH, UK

The Publishers regret that they can enter into no correspondence upon this matter.

The Woodland Trust
Osprey Publishing supports the Woodland Trust, the UK's leading woodland
conservation charity.

www.ospreypublishing.com
To find out more about our authors and books visit our website. Here you will find
extracts, author interviews, details of forthcoming events and the option to sign-up
for our newsletter.

CONTENTS

PIKE AND SHOT TACTICS
1590–1660

INTRODUCTION

For I rest out of doubt of this, if the ancient were joyned to these our new found armes, and withall the true marshalling of Bands and kinde of embattailing used, the old and new World would shortly be subject to one man. (From *De Militia Romana* by Justus Lipsius, professor at the University of Leiden, translated by Captain John Bingham,1623)

The 'pike and shot' era in European warfare, which may be taken to run from the end of the 15th century through to the beginning of the 18th century, is the period when infantry were armed with a combination of pikes and gunpowder firearms, but this covers too many years and too many changes in military technology and tactics to cover in a single book. This study describes the tactics of a distinct period within that era: specifically, from the military reforms of the Dutch leader Maurice of Nassau, Prince of Orange, in the 1590s, to the conclusion of the European wars of the first half of the 17th century, with the Peace of the Pyrenees between France and Spain in 1659 and the disbanding of the English army after the restoration of the Stuart monarchy in 1660.

Our starting point, Prince Maurice's reforms, represents a distinct advance, but not a complete break with existing military practice. Maurice's reforms worked because they combined the successful evolutionary developments of the Spanish army during the 16th century with revolutionary new ideas that reinterpreted classical Roman, Hellenistic and Byzantine military theory and practice in a practical way for a modern age and modern armies.

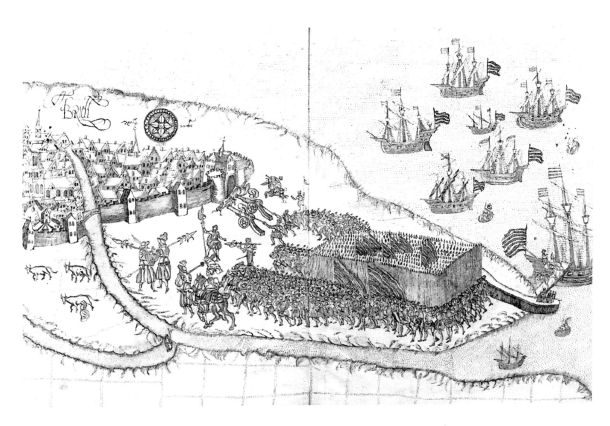

There was a long history of debate in Western Europe over the potential opportunities that a revival of the skills of the legendary armies of Macedon or Rome could offer, and this had intensified during the revival of interest in the classical past during the Renaissance. A military prince or an ambitious *condottiere* could easily imagine the advantages, and dream of being a new Alexander or Julius Caesar. From a more practical perspective, the increasing impact on the battlefield of modern Swiss, German and Spanish infantry armed with pikes made comparisons with the classical Macedonian phalanx more relevant to contemporary warfare.

The problem facing both military theorists and professional officers in the 16th century was not that they were ignorant of the classical past or that they lacked the vision to understand classical ideas in a modern context. The texts that they read certainly provided the core principles of classical infantry training; but most did not include the practical detail they needed to rediscover exactly how it actually worked. What they needed was a book that did not assume a detailed level of knowledge of the mechanics of classical military practice – basic drill and unit manoeuvre – and at first they did not have access to such a source.

The key texts that provided this practical information were translations of two less well-known titles: Claudius Aelianus' *Tactica*, and the Byzantine Emperor Leo VI's *Tactica* which drew upon it. Combined with descriptions of Roman Republican practice from Titus Livy's *Historia* and Julius Caesar's *Gallic War*, these works – with their practical explanations of unit drill – provided the basis for the new Dutch battalion (whose size was based on that of the Roman cohort), and for the adaptation of the Roman *triplex acies* battle order of three supporting lines of infantry units. This combination of ideas led Maurice to reform the Dutch army into smaller, more flexible

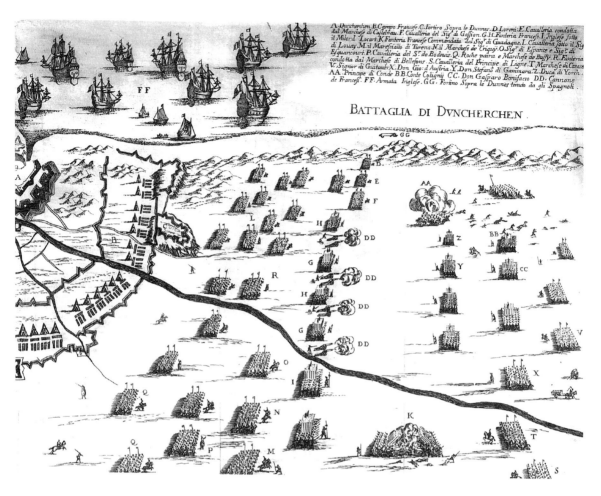

Battle of the Dunes, 14 June 1658: an Italian engraving of the decisive victory achieved outside Dunkirk by Turenne's French (left) over a Spanish army. Each side included allied English regiments, with New Model Army infantry fighting alongside the French, and exiled English Royalists under the Duke of York with the Spanish.

tactical units with new styles of tactical deployment, employing the new firing systems that he introduced to better exploit the potential of infantry firearms.

Spanish and Italian commanders – and German commanders who copied the Spanish practice, or used similar models – were not initially convinced by the new Dutch tactics, but the Dutch victory over the Spanish at Nieupoort in 1600 was a clear demonstration that they actually worked. The Swedish military system, which expanded upon the Dutch battalion system for its own unique brigade structure, provided another conclusive example by its victory at Breitenfeld in 1631, and by the following year the Imperial commander Albrecht von Wallenstein had adopted a linear army deployment based on the Dutch model. The end result was a new German doctrine that was a composite of the Dutch and Swedish, and by the 1640s this had been adopted by all sides in the Thirty Years' War (1618–48). A series of wars involving England, Scotland and Ireland – the Bishops' Wars between England and Scotland (1639–40), the Irish Revolt against English rule (1641–53), and the English Civil Wars (1642–51) – show the same process of change, as Dutch, Swedish and German styles of warfare interacted over a shorter period. By 1643 the composite German style had become the model used by all sides in the English Civil Wars.

The perspective of contemporary generals on the theory and practice of the composite German style born during the Thirty Years' War is described in the next chapter. The following chapters then describe the sequence of change and continuity through the Spanish and the French Huguenot systems in the 1590s, and the Dutch and Swedish military reforms, that gave birth to that German composite system

THE CONTEMPORARY GENERAL'S PERSPECTIVE

In the late 16th century the war in the Low Countries (modern Holland and Belgium) between the Spanish and the Dutch rebels was dominated by siege warfare rather than open-field battles. However, both sides recognized that despite the importance of sieges it was also necessary to have an effective manoeuvre force that could credibly challenge its opponents in the open field. Credibility was the key point: if it was to raise a siege, the relieving army must represent a credible threat to the besiegers. The English officer John Bingham, who had served in the Dutch army, summarized this with the comment that 'he who is master of the field, may dispose of his affaires as he listeth, hee may spoyle the Enemies Country at his pleasure, he may march where he thinketh best, he may lay siege to what Towne he is disposed, he may raise any siege that the Enemy hath layed against him. Nor can any Man be Master of field without Battaile.'

Although most of the victories that he won during the Dutch war of independence from Spain actually involved sieges, the greatest impact on his contemporaries achieved by the Dutch commander Prince Maurice of Orange, Count of Nassau (1567–1625), lay in his reforms in battlefield deployment, which offered an alternative to the dominance of the established practice of the Spanish army. Maurice's victory over the Spanish at Nieupoort in 1600 was the proof that his reforms had created a successful battlefield army, and the credibility this provided was the foundation of his success in siege warfare. Maurice was a cautious commander, who was concerned that a single battlefield defeat could decimate his carefully trained army and lead to Spanish victory in the war as a whole. His perspective was recorded by the English officer Sir Edward Cecil, who served with the Dutch army at Nieupoort:

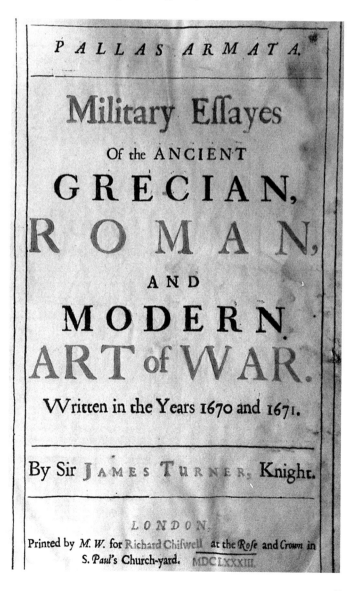

Classical influence: the frontispiece of *Pallas Armata* (1683 edition) by the Scottish mercenary Sir James Turner. The potential military advantage to be gained from an understanding of classical military theory and practice had been discussed for centuries, but it was Maurice of Nassau's reforms that first successfully combined classical doctrines with modern military realities, and his success coloured military thinking throughout the 17th century.

PALLAS ARMATA.

Military Essayes

Of the ANCIENT

GRECIAN,

ROMAN,

AND

MODERN

ART of WAR.

Written in the Years 1670 and 1671.

By Sir JAMES TURNER, Knight.

LONDON,

Printed by M. W. for Richard Chifwell at the Rofe and Crown in S. Paul's Church-yard. MDCLXXXIII.

199

Figure d'vne legion en bataille.

B B. *Sont les Manipules des Hastaires.* C C.
Celles des Princes. D D. *Celles des Triaires. Les
points qui sont autour des Manipules, representent
les Velites.*

The *triplex acies* battle line of the Republican Roman army, in an illustration from the Sieur du Praissac's *Discours Militaires*. First published in Paris in 1612, this book was the best of the early commentaries on Prince Maurice's new body of military theory and the ancient models that influenced it.

This caused the late Prince of Orange (in my hearing) when hee had fought the Battel of Nieuport: to this purpose, to direct speech unto some Hottspurrs of the French nation, that had often pressed him to give Battell. Messirs (saith hee) now you have had your desires & now you have fought a Battell, nay more, you have gained [i.e. won] a Battell. But lett mee tell you herewithall that the State hath not gotten so much as a Quart d'escu [small coin] by it; and had wee lost the Day, wee had lost all by it: Even all that my self and my Ancestors have been these three score and ten yeares a getting and preserving. And therefore Messirs, trouble mee no more hereafter, with talking to mee of Battells.

Prince Maurice's reformed Dutch army had a larger number of units, both infantry and cavalry, and the battle formations themselves were more complicated than those of the Spanish. In order to manage them successfully, Maurice brought a far higher degree of standardization and preparation to his battle planning. This provided a model that was studied and followed by other 17th-century Western European commanders, in both Protestant and Catholic armies – even down to using the same symbols as the key to annotate infantry and cavalry units on their drawn battle plans.

German mercenary infantry and cavalry in the employ of the Dutch rebel leader William of Orange, outside Roermonde on 23 July 1572. Note at top left the deep infantry columns storming the breach in the city walls.

ROERMONDE

Auriaco infesa ROERMONDA alimenta negabat,
Miles eget Cerere et Baccho, furor iste, famesqq.

Arma ministrabant, perrumpit mænia Miles,
Indomitus sceleri diro scelus addit iniquum.

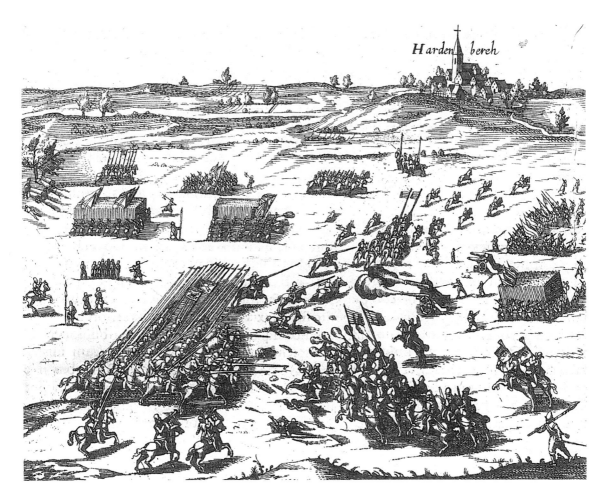

Hardenbereh

Dutch preparations

A Dutch commander, and others in this period, commonly held a parade *(paradoe)* of his army before marching out on campaign, with the practical objective of drawing his regiments together and observing their ability to deploy into battle formation and manoeuvre in open ground. The commander could then assess what his men were capable of, and adjust the complexity of his preferred battle formation accordingly. He would keep the formation simple for inexperienced soldiers, but could expect more flexibility from veteran officers and men.

Before marching a Dutch commander would decide upon his preferred formation either through discussion with his senior officers and staff, or simply by imposing it upon them. Once the decision had been made the chosen plan would be sketched out on paper by the general. The Sieur du Praissac, whose book *Discours Militaires* followed the Dutch practice, described this process in detail; the extract below is taken from the English edition translated by John Cruso and published in Cambridge in 1639:

> The Sergeant major Generall receiveth from the Generall a plat [plan] of the forms which he will give to his Armie, the disposition and placing of the members of it, Cavallrie, Infanterie, Artillerie; the order which they should observe in fight, with commission signed by the Generall to dispose it in that manner. To this commission the whole

Spanish or Italian heavy armoured lancers (left foreground) opposed to pistoliers, at Hardenberg on 16 June 1580.

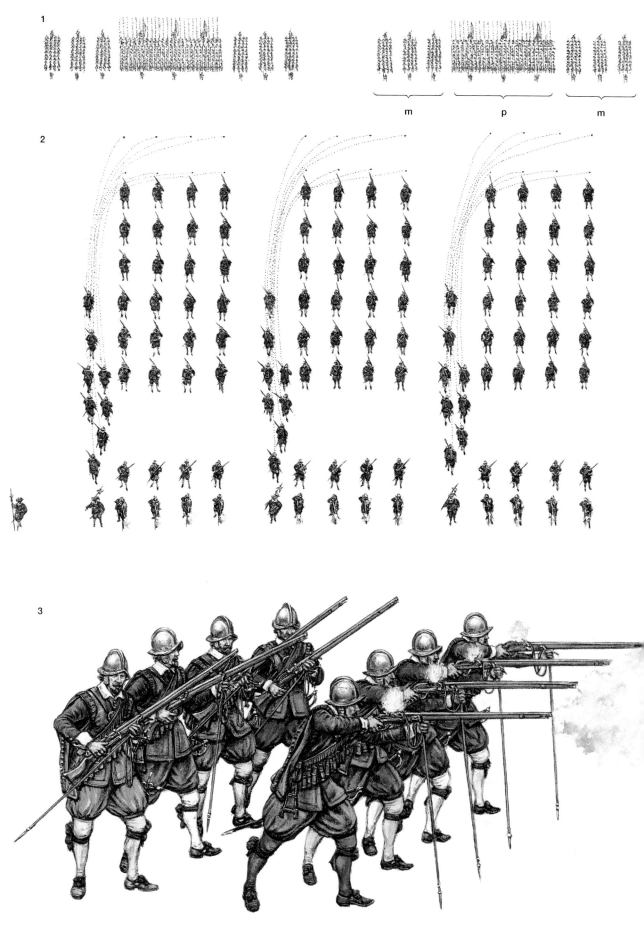

1

m   p   m

Armie must yield obedience, and the Sergeant major Generall with Marshals of the field shall dispose thereof, according to the form and place which the Generall shall have prescribed.

Several copies of the plan would be made, and officers down to the level of brigade commander (of infantry or cavalry) would receive a copy either in person at the general's council of war or via the sergeant-major general. Since an army deployed from line of march into its fighting formation brigade by brigade, every brigade commander had to understand his place in the deployment. George Monk described the objective as 'if so be your Divisions of Horse and Foot, when they march, be of the same strength as you desire to have them when they imbattelled to fight, and that you march your Divisions of Horse and Foot by Brigades as you do intend to fight them', then the army would be 'always in a readiness to receive your Enemy'. The plan could then be amended during the campaign if events – such as reinforcements arriving, or the despatch of a large contingent on some other service – affected the composition of the army, though such a variation on the original plan was usually limited in scope.

Before and during the march the Dutch commander would practice full field exercises to rehearse his preferred battlefield deployments. Contemporary accounts record this practice; a good example is that of an English officer, George Waymouth, who served in the Dutch army in the expedition to Julich in 1610, and who included in his account maps of the battle formations practiced on different days. Waymouth shows that in 1610 Prince Maurice had chosen to use the deployment style that placed infantry brigades in a diamond pattern, but carried out field exercises in several variations of it, so that if he adapted his plan on the day of battle his officers and men would be prepared and confident. The Scottish professional soldier Sir James Turner wrote:

In the marshalling of Regiments, Brigades, Companies, and Troops either of Horse or Foot, Commanders, must be very cautious when they have to do with an enemy, not to change the ordinary forms, for if at that time you offer to introduce any new form wherewith your men are not acquainted, you shall not fail to put them in some confusion, than which an enemy cannot desire a greater advantage. If you have a new figure of Battel in your head, be sure to accustom your Companies and Regiments very often by exercise to the practice of it, before you make use of it in earnest.

 THE DUTCH BATTALION AND FIRING SYSTEM
1: To his contemporaries, one of the most visible of Prince Maurice of Orange's reforms was the new Dutch tactical unit for infantry, which was both smaller and shallower than those used in the Spanish army. These smaller Dutch units, called 'battalions' amongst other terms, were seen as comparable to Roman cohorts, and Dutch propagandists explicitly underlined the connection with the classical Roman army and its successes. By 1610, Dutch battalions numbered about 500 men, and usually fought in pairs as shown in this illustration.
2: The new Dutch battalion offered flexibility and mutual support in its battlefield deployment, and its shallower depth of ten ranks meant that it could bring a higher percentage of its musketeers into the firing line than a deeper formation.

The next tactical obstacle was the search for a firing system to make best use of this firepower by enabling the musketeers to fire quickly in successive ranks. The first method used, in the late 1590s, was a form of countermarch, whereby the men in each rank fired and then retired down the intervals between adjacent files to reload at the rear; the next rank would then fire, and so on. Although this continued to be seen, the primary Dutch firing system from the early 17th century saw musketeers formed into lateral blocks of three to six files, called 'divisions'; after firing each rank retired as shown, down the interval between divisions, rather than between the individual files.
3: This shows Dutch musketeers c. 1626 in two successive ranks, in the 'ready' and 'firing' stances.

You may see this figure more largely and more exactly in my book of Cavalry, in figure 16.

Two of several diamond-pattern deployments (white blocks) practised by the Dutch army on its march to the siege of Julich in 1610. This is from the English edition of Praissac's *Discours Militaries;* the English translator, John Cruso, also wrote a cavalry manual, hence the marginal note.

Swedish aggressiveness

Prince Maurice clearly understood the concept and the consequences of decisive battle, but preferred to avoid the risk if he could. The military theory and practice arising during the Thirty Years' War, which saw the impact of the Swedish tactical style and formed the composite German style, was characterized by an equally clear view of the potential for seeking campaign solutions through decisive battles, but also by a greater appetite for risk. Gustavus Adolphus' victory at Breitenfeld, and the consequent reputation that attracted allies for his campaigns in Germany, was an example that inspired a generation of generals. These included several of those who fought in the English Civil War, such as the Royalist Prince Rupert and the New Model Army's cavalry commander, Oliver Cromwell. Jean t'Serclaes, Count Tilly, had previously demonstrated the advantages of battlefield solutions by his victories at the battle of White Mountain in 1620, which brought Bohemia under his control, and at Lutter in 1626, which broke the Danish army of King Christian IV. But Gustavus Adolphus was an altogether more inspiring figure; he defeated Count Tilly, and when he was killed at the battle of Lützen in 1632 he was at the height of his fame.

The Earl of Orrery, writing after the English Civil War, summarized the contemporary perspective on the impact of decisive battles:

All who have commanded Armies, or written on the Military Art have universally agreed, That no one Act of War, is so great in itself, or in the Consequences of it, as Fighting a Battel; since the winning of one, has not only been the cause of taking a Place besieged, (if the Army is defeated which comes to relieve it) but also by the gaining of the Victory, a Province, nay a Kingdom has often been the Reward of the Victorious. But, as the advantages are eminent to him who wins it; so the Prejudices are no less to him who loses it; and therefore nothing ought to be more exactly consider'd and weigh'd in War, than whether a decisive Battel shall be given, before the resolution to fight is taken.

The potential risk of battle was self-evident, but, compared with Prince Maurice, leading generals in the Thirty Years' War and the English Civil Wars were more willing to take that risk.

The German doctrine of the 1640s

The composite German style was described by the Imperialist officer Raimondo Montecuccoli in his manuscript *Sulle Battaglie*, written while he was a prisoner of war and completed by 1642 (Montecuccoli had fought at Breitenfeld as a cavalry officer):

> Nowadayes all captain are accustomed to arraying their troops in more than one line, a tactic which the Germans call treyfach. This is what the Imperials did at Lutzen, Soultz, Nordlingen Wittstock, Freburg and everywhere else except for Tilly in the battle of Breitenfeld-Leipzig. The latter placed his whole army along a single front and found himself in a bad way as a result.

The Earl of Orrery, whose service had been in Ireland, described this model in more detail:

> A General must never bring all his Troops to fight at once; and therefore is still to draw up his Army in two Lines or orders of Battel, and three in case the Ground, and the Number of his Forces, allow it. For those Lines are in effect, so many Armies; and the second Line being intire, though the first should be broken, often recovers the day; especially if the second line be at so just a distance behind the first, as if the first be overthrown, it does not disorder the second; and also so near that some Squadrons of the second Line, can come up timely enough to redress any beginning of a breach in the first, without too much discomposing itself.

While the examples in Orrery's *A Treatise of the Art of War* divided infantry into two or three lines, Sir James Turner, who served extensively in Germany, wrote that although 'The manner was in many places, and still is in some, to marshal Armies in three distinct Bodies, one behind another, the

Infantry distances: the uniformity introduced by the Dutch set specific frontages for each infantryman, and specific methods to change them. This illustration from John Bingham's *The Tactiks of Aelian*, published in London in 1616, shows two methods of reducing the frontages – 'Closing to the middell' and 'Closing to ye right hand/ left hand'.

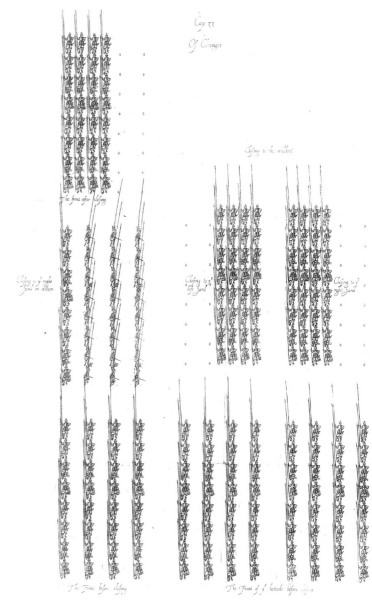

Heavy cavalry, *c.* 1616:
an armoured cuirassier or
Reiter, armed with two large
wheel-lock horse pistols and
carrying a sword as his
secondary weapon.

first was called the Vanguard, the second the Battel, the third the Reere-guard',
it was becoming more common to use two lines: 'Armies for the most part
now are marshal'd in two distinct Bodies the Van-guard and the Arreer-guard
which are commonly called Battel and Reserve'. The examples which Turner
uses also treat brigades differently. Whereas previously an army formed
on the Dutch model fought in three large brigades, it was becoming more

common to combine several weak regiments into battlefield units that were essentially battalions, but were often referred to as 'brigades'. Using this model, Turner's examples of deployments in two lines were based on a first line of four brigades and a second line of three. The origin of this revised use of the term 'brigade' and their use as distinct battlefield units is probably the result of Swedish influence.

The supporting field artillery was typically placed in pairs of guns along the front of the army, with lighter pieces associated more closely with the infantry, since these 'regimental guns' could now keep pace with advancing infantry. This was not an absolute rule, however, and larger battery groups could be formed.

The same principles and formations that were used for large armies in the field were used in miniature by smaller forces, by reducing the numbers of men in the battalions of infantry or squadrons of cavalry. The battlefield formation was based on the flexibility of a number of units deployed so that they could support one another, and the officers and soldiers had been trained to fight in that way. In order to maintain that flexibility, the general required a certain minimum number of units; to achieve this with a small force he needed to reduce the number of men in each unit rather than having a smaller number of stronger units. (An example of an English army fighting in Ireland in 1642 and deployed in this way with a number of small units is illustrated on page 56.)

Dutch heavy cavalry at Tournhout, where Prince Maurice defeated a Spanish, Walloon and German army on 24 January 1597; this detail is from an engraving in *The Commentaries of Sir Francis Vere* published in London in 1657, but is based on an earlier Dutch engraving. It shows deep formations of Dutch cavalry, in seven files and eight ranks; Maurice later reduced the depth to five ranks, giving a frontage increased to as many as 15 files. Each sub-unit is shown as being led by an officer followed by two trumpeters, with two cornets carrying standards in the front rank.

Battle of Nieupoort, 2 July 1600, in an engraving from *The Commentaries of Sir Francis Vere*. Prince Maurice's victory over a Spanish army was seen throughout Protestant Europe as proof that his military reforms worked. Compare the smaller Dutch units at upper left with the larger Spanish infantry formations at centre right.

The choice of terrain

Having decided to take the risk of battle, professional competence in deployment was seen as critical, and this was based on an understanding of the advantages of the ground as well as the battle formation selected: 'the Ranging of an Army in Battel to the very best advantage, is a great furtherence to the winning of the Victory, but the doing of it depends much, not only on the Wisdom and Skill of the General, the Nature of the Ground, and the Quality of his own Forces, but also on those of his Enemies, and of the disposition of him who commands them.'

The battle formations which a general had decided upon were likely to be adapted by circumstance, but not fundamentally altered, provided he could find the ground he needed on which to use them. The Duke of York recorded in his memoirs of service in the French army at Mont St Quentin that 'there [Maréchal Turenne] resolv'd to expect the Enemy, who came on with great joy, as knowing the advantage they had over us, both in numbers and by getting us into a plaine feild, where wee could neither retreat from them, nor avoid fighting, if they pleas'd to engage us'. In looking for a place to commit his army to battle the commander would take care to ensure that he or a trusted officer viewed the ground he would fight over or actively looked for the ground he wanted – 'with great diligence to view so well the Field you will fight in, as when you have drawn up your Army on it, you may not afterward alter the Order of it or change your Ground; for all such Mutations in the Face of your Enemy are very dangerous'.

Where possible a commander who chose to wait on the defensive would seek to secure one or both his flanks with some obstacle, as Sir James Turner commented: 'in time of Battel it is almost impossible for a Battalion or Body of either Horse or Foot to stand when it is charg'd both in front and flank, and this is ordinarily done by overwinging, so that the strongest in number has the advantage, which the weaker should endeavour to counterbalance by art, policy, and stratagem'. Where a commander was advancing upon his opponent 'drawn up in Battel [formation], ready to receive him, he will do himself an injury to march forward, for it is not to be fancied, that his adversary will be so courteous as to permit him to marshal his army, but will take his advantage and fall upon him before he can draw up his Van'. In these circumstances the commander would draw up his army into its battle formation at a distance from his opponent, and only then march it forward. This precaution was practiced by the Dutch in their field exercises and during their marches so that they could easily and quickly undertake it on campaign.

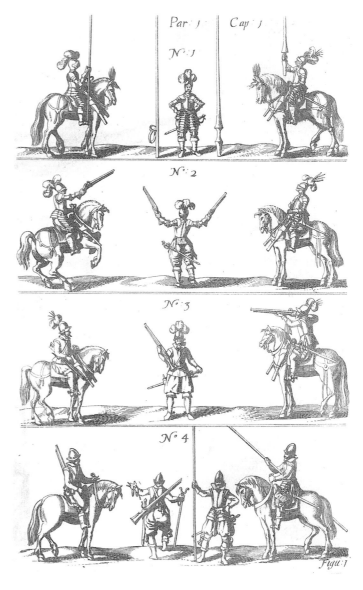

Cavalry and dragoons, *c.* 1616, from a 1635 edition of Johann Jacobi von Walhausen's *Kriegs-Kunst zu Pferd* ('The Art of War on Horseback'). From top to bottom: lancers, pistoliers, arquebusiers, and mounted infantry – dragoons.

CAVALRY

While the main cavalry was positioned on the wings of the infantry, in two or three lines, there was a strong contemporary preference to combine the effects of cavalry and infantry, and there were two main ways to achieve this. The first was the Swedish tactic of adding detachments of 'commanded' musketeers – typically in *plottons* of 50 men, but sometimes stronger – and light artillery to support the cavalry wings. This slowed down the cavalry to the pace of their infantry support; as George Monk wrote, 'if you fight [deploy] Foot amongst your Horse, your Foot must advance with your Horse, and your Horse by no means to advance before your Foot, until your Enemies Horse be put to flight'. However, these infantry detachments provided a deadly counter to the *caracole* of pistol-armed cavalry – cavalrymen firing by successive ranks – since the musket had a longer range. The second method was to place cavalry squadrons behind the infantry lines. This was originally a Dutch tactic, with cavalry deployed behind the first line of infantry; but the Swedish took it a stage further at Breitenfeld in 1631, placing supporting cavalry squadrons behind both the first and second of their two lines of infantry. German Imperial armies later copied this tactic.

The contemporary view was that small squadrons of cavalry could have an impact out of all proportion to the numbers deployed; Montecuccoli wrote that 'a small squadron of cavalry, acting promptly can wreak great havoc amongst large infantry battle lines'. The advantage this gave was that the infantry formation adopted for fighting other infantry – a centre of pikemen with wings of musketeers – was vulnerable to cavalry attack, while the square or oblong formations that infantry adopted to defend themselves against cavalry made compact targets for enemy musketeers and light artillery. The usefulness of small supporting cavalry squadrons amongst the infantry was such that commanders of the Thirty Years' War would deploy some of their best cavalry in this role.

The general would typically place his cavalry with one wing stronger than the other, and might see this as the means to deliver a decisive blow. As George Monk wrote, 'if you have one wing of Horse that are more confident in their Valour and Resolution than you are of the other, let that wing of Horse charge first (for as many hands make light work, so the best hands make surest work) and the other wing of Horse kept even with the main body of Foot until the Enemies Horse come up to charge them'. The key to success then lay in the ability of the cavalry to exploit their victory and not waste it. Monk again: '[If] either of your wings of Horse do put to flight either of your Enemies wings of Horse, to send three divisions of Horse after them ... and all other Horse that have put the Enemies wing of Horse to flight, ought to charge the Enemies Foot with as much speed as they can'. The pursuing cavalry kept their defeated opponents from rallying, and the reserve cavalry of the victorious wing would now co-operate with their own infantry by attacking the opposing infantry line in the flank.

The size and depth of cavalry squadrons differed, and Montecuccoli, writing c. 1642, described the different armies' cavalry units thus: 'Nowadays [the French] form large squadrons 7 to 8 men deep, the Dutch give their squadrons a depth of 5 so that the front turns out to have 15. In the Imperial army the squadrons are 200–250 horse or 300 horse', with a depth of 'five and sometimes four'. The Swedish 'also form squadrons of 200 to 300, the depth is but three'.

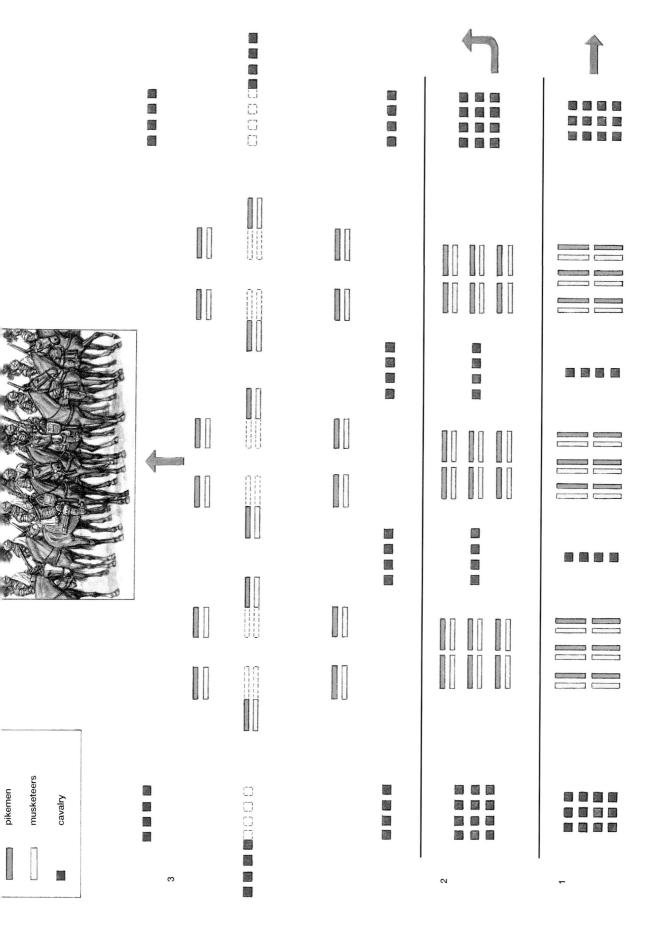

pikemen

musketeers

cavalry

1

2

3

THE INFANTRY CONFRONTATION

Sir James Turner – who had fought in several – described an infantry advance thus:

> Your advance upon an Enemy, in what posture soever he be, should be with a constant, firm and steady pace; the Musketeers (whether they be on the Flanks or interlin'd with either the Horse or the Pikes) firing all the while; but when you come within Pistol-shot [the term used here as a measure of distance], you should double your pace, till your Pikes closely serr'd together, charge these, whether Horse or Foot, whom you find before them. It is true, the business very oft comes not to push of Pike, but it hath and may come oft to it, and then Pikemen are very serviceable.

Although Turner favoured a steady advance with musketeers firing as they came (which would have required them to employ the practice of firing by successive ranks), other commanders preferred the Swedish tactic of reserving their fire until very close range, firing one or two massive volleys, and then 'falling on' opposing infantry while they were still reeling from the shock. This reserving of fire could be employed both offensively and defensively.

A good contemporary description of Scottish infantry fighting in the Swedish army at Breitenfeld was given by LtCol Muschamp to Dr William Watts: 'First (saith he), giving fire unto three little Field-pieces that I had before me, I suffered not my muskettiers to give their volleyes till I came within Pistoll-shot of the enemy, at which time I gave order to the first [three] rancks to discharge at once, and after them the other three: which done we fell pell mell into their ranckes, knocking them downe with the stocke of the Musket and our swords.' Sir James Turner – who was not present at this battle – wrote of the use of the 'Salvee' (volley) that he thought that it was used 'when either the business seems to be desparate, or that the Bodies are so near, that the Pikemen are almost come to push of Pike, and then no other use can be made of the Musquet but of the Butt-end of it'. Muschamp also described an occasion when opposing pikemen were less enthusiastic to advance, and a 'brave commander of theirs all in scarlet and gold lace there was right before us; whom we might discerne to lay upon his own mens pates [heads] and shoulders; to cut and slash divers of them, with his sword, because they would not come upon us. This gentleman maintained the fight a full houre, and more against us; but he being slaine, wee might perceive their pikes and colours [flags] to topple downe, to tumble and fall crosse one over another; whereupon all his men beginning to flee, wee had the pursuit of them until the night parted us.'

Where the battalions in the first line of an army – or part of them – are forced back, 'then the Reserve behind should be order'd immediately to advance, and encounter the Victorious Enemy, who will hardly be able to withstand that fresh charge, for it may be almost received as a Maxim, That a Troop, Regiment or Brigade, how strong so-ever it be, which hath fought with and beaten that Body of equal number that stood against it, may be easily routed by a Troop, Regiment or Brigade that has not fought, though far inferior in number. If any part of an Army get the Victory of those who stand against it, he who commands that part ought to send some Troops in pursuit of the routed Enemy, and with the rest fall on the flank of the Battallion which stands next him, and yet keeps ground. The neglect of this duty lost the famous General, Count Tili, the Battel of Leipsick [Breitenfeld-Leipzig].'

Two examples during the English Civil War – at Edgehill in 1642 and Naseby in 1645 – show this in practice, where the second lines advanced after parts of the first line were overwhelmed. When the battalions of the first line were defeated but relieved by the advance of the second line, the former's officers were expected to try to rally their men behind the second line; 'though rallying at so near a distance is not frequently seen, yet it is not banish'd out of the Modern Wars, or Armies'.

Defence by infantry against cavalry. Formed infantry armed with a combination of pike and musket could withstand cavalry, as the pike could keep riders at a distance, and the musket had a longer range and greater penetration than a cavalryman's pistol. The length of the cavalryman's lance is exaggerated in this engraving, in comparison with that of the pike.

Command and control

Communications in this period were too slow to be effective on a battlefield where each commander sought a possibly fleeting opportunity to exploit the weak points in his opponent's deployment. Thus constrained, the army commander had to build his tactical tricks into his initial deployment, so that he could bring his subordinates into play as the occasion arose. The position of the general himself was at his own discretion. Sir James Turner wrote that 'Many have reason enough to think that the General himself should stand in the middle of the Infantry of the Battel, where he useth to march, but that is not constantly practis'd, yea and but seldome in our late Wars, for many times he who commands in chief takes his station in the right Wing of the

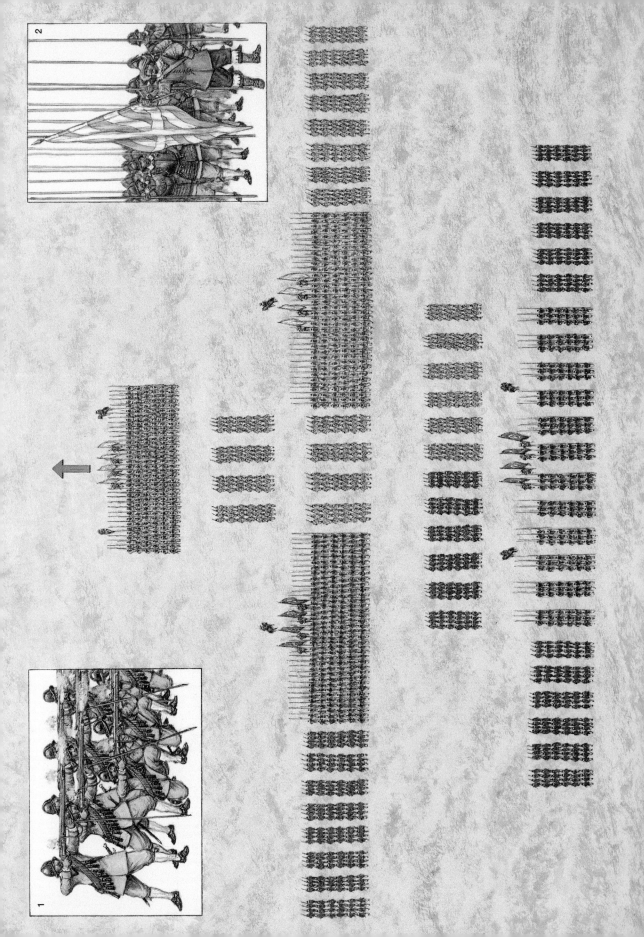

Cavalry; so did the Great King of Sweden [Gustavus Adolphus] at the first battle of Leipsick [Breitenfeld], and so did he at Lützen likewise: So did count Tilly at that same Battel at Leipsick, and so did Banier at Woodstock [Wittstock]'. By the second quarter of the 17th century a common choice for a general who did not want to command one of his cavalry wings was to position himself between his right wing cavalry and his infantry.

Apart from the difficulty of communication, a lengthy battle meant a battlefield shrouded in smoke from musketry and artillery. Here the general's skill lay in the management of chaos through the tactical possibilities that he had built into his deployment, the training and field manoeuvres he had practised with his army, and his ability to appoint subordinate officers to whom he could safely delegate local battlefield authority. The impact of the smoke of battle can be seen in accounts from both sides at the battle of Breitenfeld. An Imperialist commander wrote that 'I verily believed that I had defeated my enemy, and that victory was ours: I not knowing that our left wing was so miserably defeated. And this mistake was by reason of the great smoake; for we could not possibly see about four paces before us'. On the Swedish side, the Scottish officer Robert Munro wrote that the 'smoake being great, the dust being raised, we were as in a darke cloude, not seeing the halfe of our actions, much lesse discerning, either the way of our enemies, or yet the rest of our Briggads: whereupon, having a drummer by me, I caused him beate the Scots march, till it cleared up, which collected our friends unto us, and dispersed our enemies being overcome'. The perspective on the general's position was summarized by Orrery:

> I am fully of the opinion that the greatest Captain that ever was, or will be, is not, or can be, of himself sufficient to redress all Disorders, and lay hold of all Advantages, in an instant, when Armies are once engaged. The utmost he can do is choose well the Field of Battel; to draw up his Army according thereunto, to most Advantage; to give his General Orders, and to give the best Orders wherever he is in Person. But he cannot be Ubiquitary [everywhere at once] nor send Orders to every place enough to have them obey'd successfully. And therefore it is indisputably necessary, that he have under him, expert Chief Officers, at the Head of all Gross Bodies who may supply what is impossible for him singly to command; soe he can be well obey'd but to the time he

C **THE SWEDISH BRIGADE, 1630**
The Swedish brigade system was based upon the Dutch, but its battlefield deployment was different. This illustration shows the similarity with a Dutch or Danish brigade deployed in the diamond pattern shown in Plate B; but while Dutch brigades deployed their battalions so that each formed part of the three lines of infantry, Swedish brigades fought as complete units, and each of their two battle lines was formed from complete separate brigades. The Swedish brigade might consist of either three or four 'squadrons' (battalions); the four-squadron version is illustrated here, after an example in Dr William Watts' *The Swedish Discipline* published in London in 1632. Dr Watts recorded that he obtained his information from 'Lord Rhees' (Donald MacKay, Lord Reay), who raised a Scots regiment which served first in the Danish army and was then re-trained for Swedish service.

Each squadron consisted of about 500 men, the same number as a Dutch battalion. In theory each squadron was formed out of four infantry companies, so a four-squadron brigade could be formed from two complete regiments – here, a blue-uniformed and a yellow-uniformed regiment – since each regiment had eight companies. In practice, however, some regiments had more than eight companies, and most companies were understrength when on campaign. Brigades were not permanent formations, and the general's primary concern was to form his battle line with tactical units of approximately equal strength.

Inset 1: Musketeers deployed in three ranks to deliver the Swedish 'salvee'.
Inset 2: Ensign and pikemen.

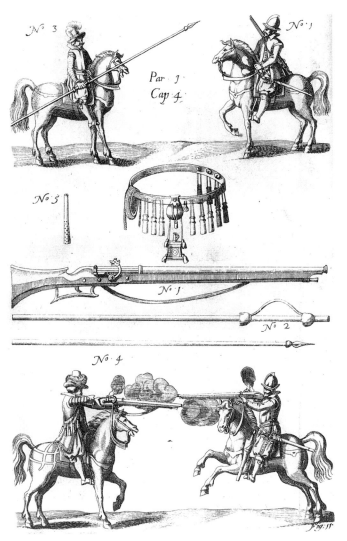

sends his Troops to the charge: after that, those only who lead them, and are with them, can actuate them according to the General Orders, or as the occasion requires, which those under him must have the judgement to lay hold of, as it were in the twinkling of an Eye; so short are the moments to acquire the victory.

Broken-ground fighting

There were also occasions when the nature of the ground was so difficult that the general's plan was inoperable, an example being the first battle of Newbury in 1643 during the English Civil War. In this case the Parliament army was intercepted as it marched back to London after relieving the siege of Gloucester, and had no choice over the ground it had to fight over. The southern sector of the battlefield was open enough to allow the deployment of infantry and cavalry in the usual way; but the central and northern sectors were broken by enclosures and hedgerows, and the Parliament colonels who wrote a report on the battle commented that in the northern sector cavalry 'could not be engaged but in small parties by reason of the hedges'.

The infantry fighting over enclosed ground fenced by hedgerows were usually musketeers, and one tactic was to take

Mounted infantry or dragoons, c. 1616. Dragoons were usually musketeers, and Walhausen's idea of mounting pikemen was not generally followed. In the central detail of weapons, note that the musket has a sling attached to the left side. The origin of the term dragoon is traced to the Dutch *dragen* or *tragen*, which translates as 'to carry'. The left man in the bottom pair is a dragoon; the other, with the saddle pistols, is an arquebusier.

one enclosure that could then be occupied and used to flank the opposing musketeers fighting in the other fields. The advantage in this form of fighting (with its pre-echoes of the Normandy *bocage* in 1944) belonged to the more experienced musketeers. Sir James Turner commented that in 1648, when the Scots army invaded England, he favoured the route through Yorkshire rather than Lancashire 'and for this reason only, that I understood Lancashire was a close country, full of ditches and hedges, which was a great advantage the English would have over our raw and undisciplined musketeers, the Parliament's army consisting of experienced and well trained sojers and excellent firemen; on the other hand Yorkshire being a more open country and full of heaths, where we might make use of our horse, and come sooner to push of pike'.

OUTPOST WARFARE

Formal battles, large or small, were only an infrequent part of campaigning, and the most common activity was raiding the quarters of opposing troops, particularly cavalry – described as 'Beating up Quarters'. George Monk wrote that 'It is very fit a General should often command his Horse and Dragoons to fall upon his Enemies outermost Horse-Quarters. The which is one of the readiest, easiest and securest ways that I know to break an Enemies Army.'

This type of action was carried out at night or in the early hours of the morning, and could sometimes involve large numbers of men; one such was the Parliament commander Sir William Waller's successful attack on the winter quarters of a Royalist brigade at Alton on 13 December 1643, and another was the unsuccessful attack on the overnight quarters of MajGen John Lambert's cavalry brigade by Scots cavalry and dragoons at Hamilton on 30 November 1650. Usually, however, these missions were smaller raids by a few troops of cavalry on a static garrison, or the outlying quarters of a marching army as it advanced or retreated. This was an everyday feature of military activity, and the optimum way of carrying out this type of raid was included in cavalry training manuals. The description in John Cruso's, and that in John Vernon's (which is based on Cruso), described the use of cavalry only, but it was common to support the attack with musketeers – provided either by dragoons or by infantry temporarily mounted or riding double behind cavalrymen. Dragoons or other musketeers would be useful in house-to-house fighting in the enemy quarters themselves, as well as providing firepower support for cavalry actions.

Essentially, the attackers' objective was to cut down the enemy sentries before an alarm could be given and then overrun the *corps de gard*, who 'must be armed all night, and have their horses at hand, readie and bridled'. They would then seek to take control of the 'alarme point' (the area designated for troops in quarters to muster in the case of an alarm), and any other large open space where the enemy garrison might gather to organize themselves, such as the 'market place'. Cruso described the alarm point as 'that place without [i.e. outside] the village, where the souldiers are to assemble to withstand an assailing enemy, being a place of great consequence'. The commander of the quarter would have given advance instructions in case of an attack, and 'appointeth a certain place for every troop, where they shall stand, which way faced'. By sending a troop to ride through the streets the attacking cavalry kept

Field artillery piece, 1612: an illustration from Praissac's *Discours Militaires*. The Dutch introduced lighter 3-pdr cannon called 'drakes' in the 1620s, but it was the Swedish who made best use of light guns to accompany their infantry. So-called 'leather' cannon were used briefly during Gustavus Adolphus' campaigns in Poland in 1627–29; the barrel was actually made of thin copper, bound with wire and covered with leather, but it could only take a relatively light charge due to the risk of bursting. They were soon replaced with more conventional cast-bronze 3-pdr regimental guns.

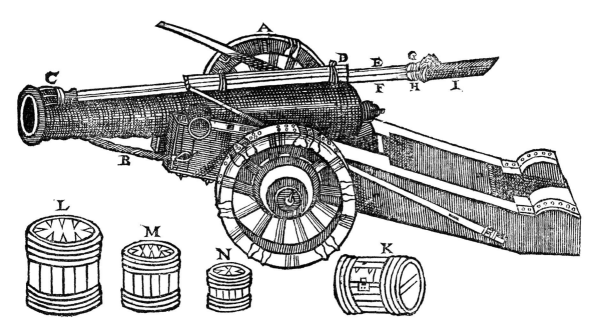

their opponents in small groups, which could then be killed or captured while isolated. Lastly, when the surprised occupiers gave up the struggle and sought to escape, a troop waiting outside the quarters would intercept them. The objective of the defending commander was to slow down the attack at all costs with his *corps de gard* and any other men he could get together quickly, in order to give the bulk of his force a chance to arm and organize themselves to resist the attack *en masse* rather than in isolated handfuls.

THE SPANISH ARMY

In the 1590s the Spanish had the leading army of their day, feared for its proven competence in a wide range of military theatres. The Spanish army saw service in Italy against the French and their Swiss mercenaries and Italian allies; in the Mediterranean, against the Ottoman Turkish empire and North African corsairs; in the Low Countries against Protestant rebels; in France in support of the Catholic League, and in the Americas. The army was Spanish in the sense that it was the army of the King of Spain, but was multinational in composition and was formed of national contingents. Its strength was in its infantry – Spanish or Italian *tercios*, and German regiments. Infantry formations had evolved during the 15th and 16th centuries into an effective and aggressive force on the battlefield, and they were the key tactical component during the Eighty Years' War in the Low Countries.

Whilst any Renaissance commander was naturally interested in the classics, and many were well-educated men who would be flattered to be compared with the great generals of antiquity, most felt that they had a workable system already, and it would take something exceptional to persuade them to change. The body of Spanish military literature of the 1580s–90s shows an evolving system of both theory and practice, respectful of classical precedent but confident in its fitness for modern warfare.[1]

Renaissance commanders also saw themselves as being at the cutting edge of modern ideas through their use of arithmetic and, to some extent, geometry in the formation of their tactical units. The 16th century saw advances in forms of fortification using mathematics to calculate frontages and angles of fire; to an extent this spilt over into tactical infantry formations, through a view that a large infantry formation was comparable to a moving fortress, with walls of men instead of stone and with outlying bodies of shot in place of bastions. This interest in mathematics led to the inclusion of mathematical tables in military books, to enable the officer to calculate the frontage which particular numbers and depths of soldiers would require and thus the ground that they could hold. In their simplest form these are genuinely useful; at worst, the tables become an end in themselves and the calculations become overly complex and impractical.

The key officer responsible for combining companies and tercios into tactical units was the *Sergento Mayor* or sergeant-major, in our period a senior commissioned officer and second in command in a tercio after the *Maestre de Campo*, whose role was particularly described in Francisco de Valdes' work

OPPOSITE TOP
Spanish infantry of the 1570s: detail from a collection of engravings of the Dutch revolt published in Amsterdam in 1622.

OPPOSITE BOTTOM
Don Fernando Alvarez de Toledo, Duke of Alva (1510–82), the first Captain-General of the Spanish Army of Flanders in 1567–73. An extremely able and determined general in Germany under the Emperor Charles V and in Italy under his son Philip II of Spain, he became infamous for the brutality of his suppression of the Dutch rebels, but was finally unable to quell the coastal raiding of the 'Sea Beggars'.

1 Key works were Francisco de Valdes' *Espeio, y deceplina militar* (Brussels, 1589); Sancho Londono's *El discurso sobre la forma de redvzir la disciplina military* (Brussels, 1589); Marcos Isaba's *Cuerpo enfermo de la milicia Espanola* (Madrid, 1594); and Bernardino de Mendoza's *Theorica y practica de Guerra* (Madrid, 1595).

Espeio, y deceplena militar. This was a technically difficult exercise; Robert Barret, an English officer who had served in the Spanish army, wrote in his book *The Theorike and Practike of Moderne Warres* (1598) that this task required an officer who was 'very skilfull in Arithmetike, for without the same, he could hardly perform his office: and not onely to know how embattle the companies of his owne Regiment, but of many Regiments together and of any number: for that many times the Generall doth command to frame a battell [single formation] of sundry Regiments together'.

The Spanish tactical unit for infantry was a large, deep body of pikemen with 'sleeves' of musketeers on each side, which could include advanced horns on either side or separate bodies of shot at all four corners. During the later 16th century the introduction of a heavy musket temporarily reduced the overall number of shot, as it was a far deadlier weapon; but the overall trend was for a steady increase in the number of shot, so by 1601 a muster of Spanish tercios in the Army of Flanders listed 1,237 musketeers and 2,117 arquebusiers [men with lighter firearms] to 1,047 armoured pikemen and 954 other pikemen.

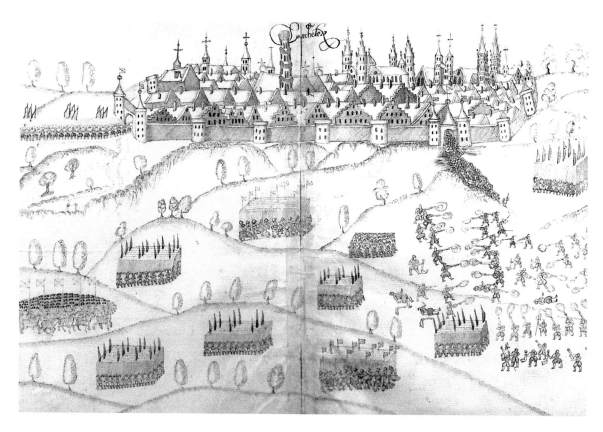

ABOVE
Spanish army at the taking of Mechlin on 17 September 1572, the occasion of infamous atrocities against the townspeople. Note the squadrons of cavalry (low left, high centre, low right); and (far right), the arquebusiers/calivermen skirmishing in loose formation. (By permission of the Warden and Fellows of All Souls College, Oxford)

OPPOSITE TOP
Another rare image of infantry deployed in loose formation – *a la disbandada*. The engraving seems to give an impression of uneven ground rolling up into woodland, which is logical: the weakness of such skirmishers was that they had no defence against cavalry, and the contemporary view that men in such loose order could be cut to pieces if caught on open ground was entirely accurate.

German infantry in Spanish service were formed in regiments with a theoretical strength of ten companies of 300 men each, half pike and half shot. Spanish commanders now considered that firepower from infantry shot and artillery was the battle-winning weapon. Don Bernardino de Mendoza wrote in his *Theortica y Practica de Guerra* (published in Madrid in 1595, and translated into English in 1597) that 'the greatest parte of victories which is gained at this time, is by having obteyned them with artillerie or readiness of harquebuserie by their livelie voleyes, disorderinge the squadrons of the enimie in such manner as they put them in rowte'. However, the Spanish still considered that a combination of shot and pike was necessary for an effective battlefield unit; Gerat Barry, an Irish officer in Spanish service, wrote in the 1630s that 'the armed [armoured] pike is the strength of the battell [battle formation], so without question, is the shot the furie of the field: but the one without the other is weakened, the better halfe of their strength'.

The infantry formation

By the 1590s two main types of tactical infantry formation were in use: the square, and the oblong with a broader front than its depth, sometimes called a bastard square. The selection of one or the other depended upon circumstance; they were 'both sufficient strong, but the difference which may happen, is to be judged according to the situation and disposition of the ground, and occasions to fight'. It was believed that the 'square of men would be best, as in open field, without advantage of hedge, ditch, water, marsh or wood, or whether the enemie is strong in horse, to charge on every side: the which the just square of men, in everie part is found to be equally strong, and apt every way to receive the charge'. Where the natural advantages of the ground favoured the Spanish,

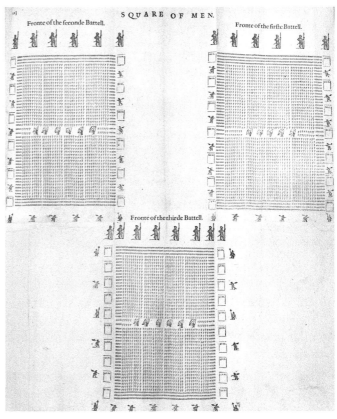

'it were better to fight in broad front, for that thereby, many hands do come to fight at once'.

When attacked by cavalry, the intention was for the shot to be protected by the length of the pikes, and 'the right and natural girdelinge of shott indeede ought to be no more shott in ranke, then that the pike may well cover and defende', this being 'three or four shott at the most'. Where the number of shot was greater than could easily be protected by the pike the tactic was to form a hollow square or oblong, with three or four ranks of shot outside and protected by the pike and the surplus shot brought inside the square.

An infantry battle formation was formed out of several companies – which could be from one or from

Deployment of three Spanish infantry 'battells', in an illustration from the Irish captain Gerat Barry's *A Discourse of Military Discipline* published in Brussels in 1634. Note the deep formations. (By permission The British Library)

Fronte of the seconde Battell.

945 pikes.
1080 musk.
2⅜ 2025.

Fronte of the firste Battell.

Fronte of the thirde Battell.

Fronte of the fifthe Battell.

Fronte of the fourthe Battell.

Table of the five Batteles.

Divisiones of the firste Battell: Firste division is 9. r. of 7. pikes. ——— 63 pikes.
Seconde division. Idem. ——— 63 pikes.
The thirde division. Alsoe. ——— 63 pikes.

Multiplied by five. ——— 189 pikes.
5.

Pikes of the five Batteles. ——— 945 pikes.
Lininge shott of the righte flanke of the firste battell of pikes, 9. rankes of musketes in 21. hr. ranks. ——— 27 musk.
Lininge shot of the lieft flank 9. r. of 3. musketes. ——— 27 musk. } 945 musk.
Lininng shot of the front 28. r. of 3. m. in each ranke. ——— 81 musk. } 1080 pikes.
Guarnison of shot of the reregarde 28. r. of 3. musketes. ——— 81 musk. } 2025 men.

Multiplied by ——— 5. 216 musk.

Lininge shott of the 5. battelles. ——— 1080.

Advertisinge that no pikes nor shot did remaine oute of the divisiones to guarnishe the culoures, so that one ranke of pikes and shott may by cutt all a longeste, the fronte or flanke of each battell to guarnish the culoure.

several tercios – by first deciding upon the depth of the formation, then separating the companies into contingents of shot and pikemen. The central body was created by forming up the pikemen of the first company to the required depth, and then forming each successive company alongside it; this ensured that men of the same company continued to serve together, with the best-equipped men in each company at the head of the files, and it probably had its origins in Swiss practice. The Spanish developed workable processes to deliver infantry firepower, although the depth of the 'sleeves' of shot alongside their pike was still wasteful. One tactic described by the English officer Robert Barret was to use small detachments or 'sundrie troupes of 30, 40 or 50 in a troupe, the one to second the other,' and to fire volleys – 'another order of discharging of troupes of Muskets in vollie, the which I have seen used by the Italian and the Spaniard'. Sir John Smythe, another

Another illustration from Barry's book, showing five Spanish 'battells'. Note the shallower formations here; the musketeers are in three-deep deployment, and the central pike block of each 'battell' is made up of three 'divisions' each of seven files of nine ranks of pikemen, totalling 189 pike to 216 shot. (By permission The British Library)

D **SWEDISH FORMATION AT PFAFFENHOFEN, 1633**

This plate is based on a contemporary engraving from *Theatrum Europaeum*, showing the deployment of a mainly German army commanded by the Swedish general Gustav Horn at the battle of Pfaffenhofen on 10 August 1633, during the Thirty Years' War, against an Imperialist army commanded by Charles of Lorraine. The deployment shows that in 1633, the year after the death of Gustavus Adolphus at Lützen, Swedish commanders retained the Swedish brigade formation for their infantry.

Horn drew up his infantry in five brigades, with three in his first line, and two in the second placed to cover the intervals between those in the first. Two squadrons of cavalry deployed in direct support of the infantry have been brought forward into these intervals (**C**); all three of the military styles of the day – Dutch, Swedish, and the later composite German – included the option of placing some cavalry to provide direct support to the infantry lines. The main cavalry deployment shows five squadrons on the right wing of the infantry and four on the left; each wing has two lines of cavalry, with those in the second line covering the intervals. Note the *plottons* of 'commanded musketeers', detached from the infantry brigades to provide the troopers with firepower support (**c, m, c, m, c**) – a Swedish tactic that later figured in the composite German style of deployment.

Inset 1: German mercenary cavalry.
Inset 2: Swedish field artillery crew.

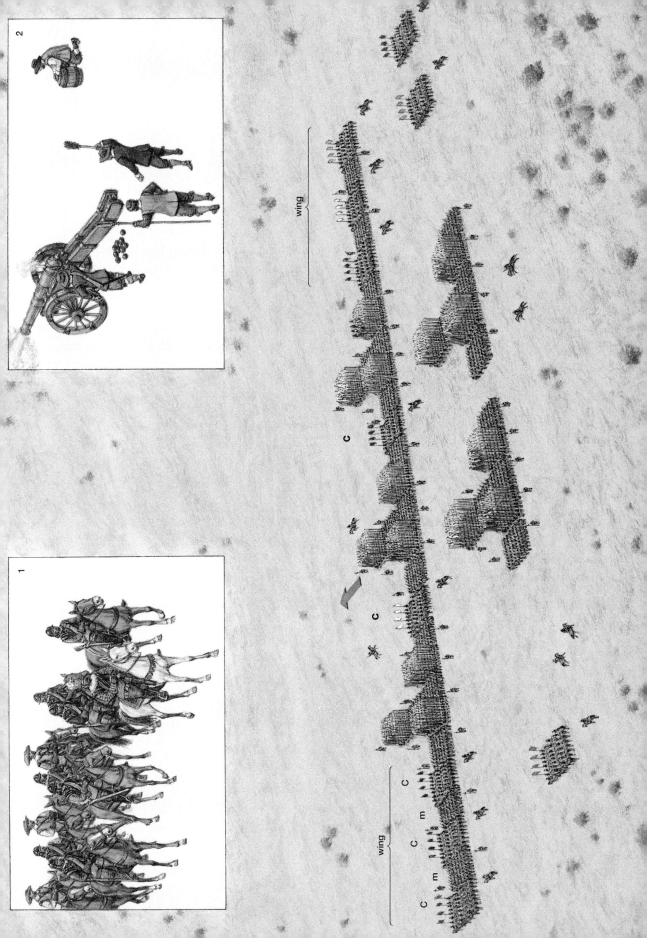

2

1

wing

c

c

c

c

m

c

c

m

wing

Englishman who had served with the Spanish army, recorded the Spanish practice of sending out skirmishing musketeers to draw enemy fire, the main body 'keeping the force of their shot, may give their whole volleys at their enemies approaching within 10, 15 or 20 paces'.

Cavalry

Spanish cavalry were not exceptional, and German mercenary horse – pistol-armed heavy cavalry *Reiters* – were hired to strengthen this arm. The main battle cavalry in the 1590s were lancers and *pistoliers*, both wearing heavy defensive armour, the latter having originated in Germany through the availability of effective wheel-lock pistols. The tactical formations of the two types were different. Like their medieval predecessors the lancers charged in line – *en haye* – while pistoliers, whose tactic was to deliver successive volleys of fire rank by rank, were formed in deeper columns.

However, experiments to develop the potential of cavalry in the 1590s were led by the French Huguenot (Protestant) armies, who used a combination of heavy pistoliers with lighter mounted arquebusiers to provide firepower support. By the battle of Ivry in 1590 the Huguenot army – now the royal army of King Henri IV – had abandoned the lance. The lighter-armed Huguenot cavalry were the result of a comparative lack of funds; since many of his supporters came from amongst the impoverished lesser French nobility, Henri of Navarre had been forced to wage war – as he said – *á la Huguenotte* – 'on the cheap'. An example was Jacques Pape, Sieur de Saint-Aubin, who wrote in his memoirs that 'I had in truth a good Arabian horse that served me very well, but I was much at a disadvantage in my weapons, having only a mere cuirass'. Huguenot armies were also particularly noted for the strategic use they made of the mobility of their cavalry forces, including the mounted arquebusiers who fought in support of the main battle cavalry, both on horseback and dismounted to provide infantry firepower support. In Henri's armies there were more mounted arquebusiers – sometimes referred to as *carabins* – than heavy battle cavalry.

THE DUTCH REFORMS

Prince Maurice's reform of the Dutch army represented a radical change in terms of the deployment of an army as a whole; in the structuring of tactical formations from a larger number of co-ordinated units; and in the introduction of more effective infantry firing systems. There was no change in the nature of the weapons and armour used to equip infantry – as pikemen, arquebusiers and musketeers – but new, standardized patterns were introduced for the Dutch army in 1599. The concept of increased standardization or uniformity runs right through the Dutch reforms, whether for military equipment or the orders given for unit manoeuvres – thus Henry Hexham, an English officer in Dutch service: 'How carefull and industrious Prince Maurice was of famous memory (the Father of Souldiers) to establish an uniforme order and Discipline amongst us'. For admirers like Hexham, Prince Maurice was the author of significant change, and his victory over the Spanish Army of Flanders at Nieupoort in 1600 provided the proof that the new Dutch system could now contend against the leading army its day, and win. Maurice's reforms were not limited to his field army and its tactics, but also focused on siege warfare. His contribution here, too, was to bring a greater degree of pragmatism, organization and uniformity to the whole exercise.

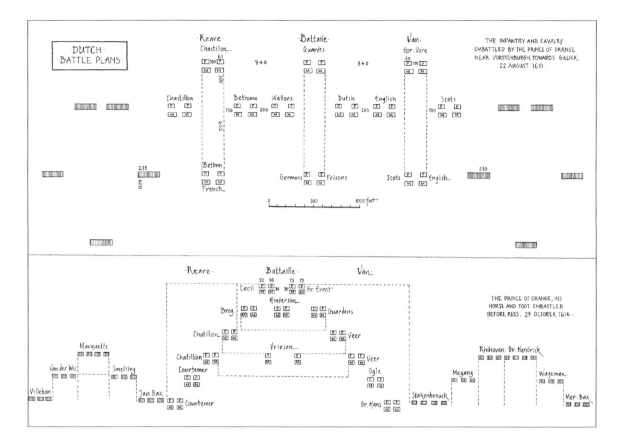

Dutch battle plans: the two types of army deployment most often used by Prince Maurice from c. 1610 – the Vanguard, Battle and Rearguard in line of diamond-shaped brigades (top); and in the wedge.

The most common form of 17th-century battlefield notation of units was a blank oblong for infantry and one shaded with vertical lines for cavalry. Originally a Dutch notation, its use spread throughout Western Europe, to Catholic as well as Protestant armies. (There is an example of the Scottish Sergeant-Major General, Sir James Lumsden, using this notation during the English Civil War.) For consistency, all re-drawn black and white battle plans in this book use this notation, with 'P' and 'M' for pikemen and musketeers.

Maurice was not the sole author of the military changes he introduced, but his position as Stadtholder and military leader of the rebel United Provinces provided the authority for the systematic introduction and practice of new ideas. As already stated, there had been increased interest throughout the 16th century in the potential offered by the Roman art of war described in translations of surviving texts, particularly Flavius Vegetius' *De re Militari* and Sextus Julius Frontinus' *Strategemata*, as well as Roman histories such as those by Julius Caesar, Livy and Polybius. Niccolo Macchiavelli, in particular, had taken this a step further by linking classical examples with his own ideas on contemporary warfare and politics in his *Libra della arte della Guerra* (Florence, 1521). The increased effectiveness of infantry firepower made the 1590s a very different world from Machiavelli's of 70 years before, but Machiavelli remained popular reading and had a profound influence on another philosopher, Justus Lipsius, professor at the University of Leiden between 1579 and 1591. Lipsius' perspective on Roman examples was published in his *De Militia Romana libri quinque, Commentarius ad Polybium* (Antwerp, 1595), but they would already have been familiar to his students and his correspondents.

There are strong comparisons between the positions of Machiavelli and Justus Lipsius, both of whom were writing at times when the security of their states was threatened by war with Spain. Both see parallels between the massive infantry formations of their day and the Macedonian phalanx of the classical past, and their reading of Livy suggested the opportunities that more manoeuvrable Roman maniples might offer. John Bingham translates Justus Lipsius as writing 'for as Livy saith, the Phalange is unmovable and of

'reserve'

one kinde, the Roman battell consisting of many parts, easie to be divided, easie to be joined and knit together, if use require'. Justus Lipsius recommended the *triplex acies* formation of three lines of infantry units as his model, using either cohorts or maniples as the units 'so placed one to second another'.[2] But like Machiavelli before him, Justus Lipsius failed to include the basic operating instructions necessary to bring the theory into practice, and neither did he fully appreciate the difference in firepower impact between classical slingers or archers and modern firearms. However, Prince Maurice and his circle were very much aware of the value of infantry firepower, and the Dutch army reforms introduced a series of new firing systems.

The Dutch battalion

The cornerstone of the new Dutch tactical formation was its infantry battalion, with a reduced depth of ten ranks. The Dutch used the terms 'battalion' and 'division' to refer to a battalion at this time, but 'division' was used by different military writers of the period to refer to different types and sizes of units. The term battalion had been in use since the early 16th century – for example, in 1521 Macchiavelli had described ten sub-units of 450 men each as *battagloni*. For the sake of clarity, 'battalion' is used in this present book to refer to a battlefield unit, and the term 'division' is used for a sub-unit within an infantry company consisting of three to six files all armed alike as pikemen or musketeers. As in the Spanish army, the Dutch battlefield units consisted of infantrymen armed either as pike or shot – the latter either arquebusiers/calivermen, or musketeers with heavier weapons requiring a musket-rest to prop them in the aiming position; the caliver was withdrawn from Dutch service in 1609, and thereafter the Dutch shot were all musketeers.

The first formal demonstration of the Dutch battalions deployed in a tactical formation was at Steenwijk following the capture of that city in 1592, but since this was a very public demonstration the training and practice to achieve it must have been carried out over several previous years. On that occasion seven battalions of Dutch infantry were deployed for a parade in a chequerboard formation, with the units in the second line covering the spaces between the units in the first. By 1610 (when the Dutch army's practice deployments during the Julich campaign were widely publicized), its battalions commonly served in

2 See Elite 172: *Roman Battle Tactics 390–110 BC*

E **ENGLISH ROYALIST FORMATION AT EDGEHILL, 1642**

This plate is based on a manuscript drawing by Sir Bernard de Gomme, a Walloon engineer officer on Prince Rupert's staff, which is a more carefully drawn version of the original 'headquarters plan' for the army's deployment. The original version would have been the rough sketch circulated amongst senior officers down to brigade level before the battle on 22 October 1642.

The Royalist infantry had originally been trained in the Dutch style, but Prince Rupert persuaded his uncle King Charles I to adopt the Swedish deployment illustrated here. The infantry have been deployed in five brigades, three in the first line and two in the second line covering the intervals in the first. The brigades themselves each consist of four squadrons/

battalions, rather than the three which King Gustavus Adolphus used at the battles of Breitenfeld and Lützen and which Horn used at Pfaffenhofen (see Plate D). Dr William Watts illustrated this four-squadron version in his book *The Swedish Discipline*; in 1642 he was Prince Rupert's chaplain, accompanying him in 'all the battles which he fought with the parliamentarians'. The commanded musketeers which form part of this brigade structure have been detached for service on the flanks of the army, and are not shown. The cavalry (**c**) is deployed in two lines, with squadrons in the second rank covering the spaces between those in the first, but there are no commanded musketeers in immediate support of the cavalry squadrons. Note the vestigial 'reserve' of horse and shot.
Top: Royalist cavalry, drawn up in three ranks; the riders with the best equipment would take their places in the first two ranks.

pairs, each battalion having an optimum strength of 500 men, half pikemen and half musketeers. The rationale of the Dutch system was set out in Hexham's *The Principles of the Art Militarie* as 'the ordering of a Regiment … namely, that Companies being made into even files, & ten deepe, foure or five Companies, ioyned together make a division …. Now the fittest number of men to make a division of, is accounted to be 500. Pikes, & Musketteires, that is, 25 files of Pikes, and 25 files of Musketteires, or more, or lesse of the one or of the other, as they fall out.'

It must be understood that the Dutch battalion was a tactical battlefield formation, not an administrative element of a regiment. In his optimum example, Hexham's Dutch regiment would provide the men for both of a pair of battalions. In practice, however, Dutch regiments did not all have the same strength either in terms of the number of companies in a regiment or the number of men in a company, and under campaign conditions strengths would vary still further. On campaign weaker regiments might only have sufficient men to form one of the paired tactical battalions, or in extreme cases it might be necessary to form two or more weak regiments into a single battalion. The concept of paired battalions was retained for the battle formation, since it was the requirements of the overall formation that were dominant.

The company

The unit of administrative organization was a regiment, comprising several companies; the company was purely an administrative entity, since it was too small to fight independently. A single regiment might be deployed as a single fighting battalion or divided into two battalions, but the dominant battlefield formation was the battalion not the regiment. However, it was recognized that the sense of distinct identity that bonded soldiers serving together in a particular company and living alongside one another in camp and on campaign was a valuable quality that should be preserved. The relationship between companies and battlefield units in the Dutch army worked on the same principle as in the Spanish, although Dutch companies and tactical units were smaller. In each case, the pike and shot of each company were separated, and then collectively formed into the battlefield units – battalions in the Dutch army – which would fight with a centre of pikemen flanked by shot on both sides. The sub-unit of a Dutch company was a 'division' of three to six files, armed alike as either pike or shot, with each file being ten deep, and even a weak company could usually muster this many soldiers. These divisions remained intact when they were combined to form the tactical battalion, thus ensuring that men from the same company fought alongside one another.

Where a strong regiment was divided into two battalions, companies were allocated to one battalion or another on the basis of the seniority of the company commander – so the colonel's and the sergeant-major's companies would be included in the right-hand battalion of the two, and the lieutenant-colonel's and first (senior) captain's companies would be amongst those forming the left-hand battalion. The allocation of the other captains' companies to the different battalions varied, but the overall principle was to spread the more senior – and thus probably more experienced – officers between both battalions rather than concentrating them in one or the other.

The actual process of forming a battalion out of several companies was straightforward, and would be carried out by the regiment's sergeant-major or, if more than one regiment was to form a single battalion, by the sergeant-major appointed by the officer commanding the battalion. The Scottish mercenary officer Turner wrote that this process 'may be done with much ease, and a few words, if the Major please; but some have the vanity to make themselves and their soldiers more business than they need to by crying this and that, riding here and there, making work for themselves, and sometimes sport to the Beholders'. Essentially, the sergeant-major would use one of two methods, both beginning with drawing up the companies that were to form the battalion in a single line alongside one another. The first method was to order all the groups of pikemen to advance about 20 paces, and then join them together to form the centre of the battalion, the musketeers then being divided to form the two wings. The second method would be used if there was no room to advance the pikemen, in which case the pike from the companies would turn to face towards the centre and then march towards that central point to form the pike body, and the shot would face outwards towards the right or left flank to which they were allocated, and march outwards to form the musketeer wings of the battalion.

In describing the advantages of the Dutch battalions over the larger Spanish infantry formations, Hexham wrote that 'This number [500 men to a battalion] being so embattailed makes an *Agile* bodie, & the best to be brought to fight, and two of them being ioyned neere one an other, can best second, and releive each other, better then your great *Phalanges*, which are

Dutch system for two 'divisions' of musketeers firing by successive ranks. The practice was to send forward two ranks, have them fire one after the other, and retire to the rear down the lane between the five-file divisions to rejoin the back of the formation to reload, while the next two marched forward. (See also Plate A.)

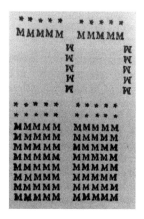

37

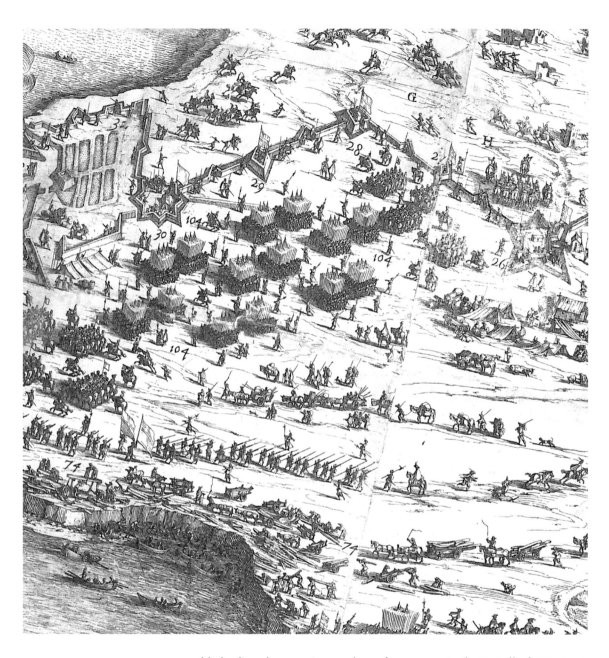

French infantry formation, 1628: detail from Jacques Callot's engraving of the siege of La Rochelle. This shows two bodies of French infantry in diamond-pattern formations – an indication of Dutch influence. (By permission The British Library)

unweeldy bodies, the experience whereof was seene in the Battell of *Nieuport:* for being once broken, & routed, they can hardly be reallyed [rallied] againe, and cannot bring so many men to Fight, as the Lesser Bodies doe.' The comparison which Hexham drew had a direct relation to Livy's description of the defeat of the Macedonian phalanx by smaller Roman units at the battle of Pydna, and this was intended to be evident to any contemporary reader. This type of parallel was deliberately and extensively publicized by the Dutch, including by their parades of battalions in battle formation. The intention was to underline the comparison of Dutch battalions with Roman cohorts and the Dutch army deployments with the Roman *triplex acies,* in order to reinforce the view that the Prince Maurice's army had successfully cracked the problem of interpreting classical military practice for a modern world, and was therefore a dangerous opponent and a useful ally.

French musketeer, from the Sieur de Lostelnau's *Le Marechal de Bataille* published in Paris in 1647. The postures are based on Jacob de Gheyn's much earlier manual, but the soldiers wear current French military costume.

The Dutch firing system

The Dutch were able to use much more effective firing systems that the Spanish for two reasons. Firstly, the main body of their shot, formed on the wings of their central pike block, was drawn up in a broader, shallower formation than their opponents, so if equal numbers of shot were opposed the Dutch could bring more men into the firing line. Secondly, the Dutch developed a much better organized firing system, whereby each rank fired successively and then retired to the rear of the musketeer body to reload; by the time all ten ranks had fired the men who had originally been in the first rank had reloaded and were ready to fire again. This rank-firing system could be used while holding ground, advancing, or retiring in the face of the enemy.

Although a musket ball would carry a lot further, the effective killing range for musket fire was considered to be around 100 to 120 yards, and

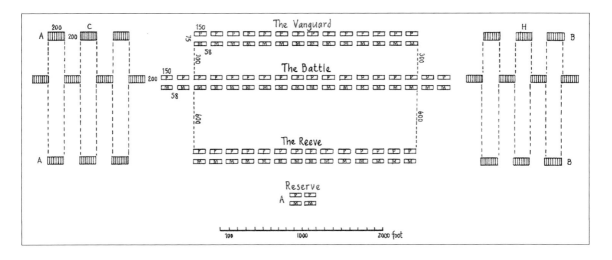

The following images were labelled within the diagram:

The Vanguard

The Battle

The Reeve

Reserve

Theoretical Dutch battle formation, from an illustration in Henry Hexham's *The Second Part of the Principles of the Art Militarie Practised in the Warres of the United Provinces*; the engraver's signature is dated 1638. The plan is for an army of 24,000 infantry deployed in three brigades, and 6,000 cavalry. This formation places each of three infantry brigades in a separate battle line.

concentrated fire would begin at this range. The Dutch firing system used two main patterns, both providing fire rank by rank. One of these employed the countermarch, whereby each musketeer fired, then turned to his right and marched down the interval between the files to the rear of the column. Although this classical drill, modified from Aelian's *Tactica*, was certainly practiced, the Dutch preferred an alternative system based on the divisions of the company – groups of three to six files. This involved the first rank firing, then facing right and marching to the rear down the intervals between divisions instead of the intervals between individual files (see Plate A). Based partly upon the existing cavalry practice of firing by *caracole,* this had the advantage that the width of the frontage remained the same, whereas in order to countermarch by files the frontage had to be doubled to provide lanes between individual files. This second system was certainly in use by 1617, as it is shown in the manual *Low-Countrie Trayning* by Capt John Waymouth (brother of George), an English officer in Dutch service.

BATTLE PLANS – THE DUTCH BRIGADE

To form a marching army for a campaign, the Dutch allocated their battalions into 'three parts called *Brigadoes*, or *Tercias*', referred to as the Vanguard, the Battle and the Rearguard. These were not the titles of permanent groupings; typically the position at the head of a Dutch army was allocated by rotation each day, and whichever brigade marched at the head of the column that day was called the Vanguard brigade. When a Dutch commander (or another, such as the Danish, who used the Dutch model) prepared for battle, he would typically deploy his army from right to left. The right-wing cavalry deployed first, and then the Vanguard infantry brigade. If the brigades were drawn up one alongside one another then the Vanguard would be the right-hand infantry brigade, with the Battle in the middle and the Rearguard on the left, and the left-wing cavalry drawn up alongside the Rearguard (see page 33, top).

Where a pitched battle – called a 'sett battle' by contemporaries – was expected, regimental precedence became important for the positioning of regiments in each of the three brigades. Professional soldiers, both officers and men, placed great value on military customs and traditions, and adherence to these supported their morale on the day of battle. In the Dutch army the position of precedence – where the senior regiment was to be found – might be

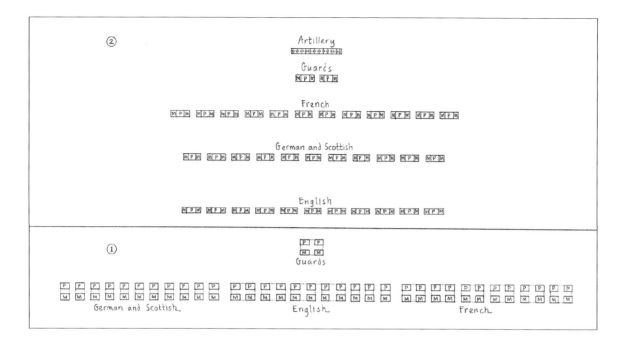

in either the Vanguard or the Battle. When battle was anticipated the army commander would arrange his order of march to suit his requirements for the coming action and to keep his regiments and their officers happy over precedence. If the commander was surprised, however, he might have to ignore precedence and march out and deploy quickly from wherever his men had camped or whatever his order of march had been.

Prince Maurice's army used three distinct types of battle formation, all of which were designed to be used offensively or defensively, and with the object that the battalions that formed them could maneuver within the formation. Within each of the three types, the army commander retained the option for some variation to take account of circumstances – such as the size of his army, or some particular tactical trick that he favoured – while maintaining the principle of that type of deployment. For example, he might make the infantry brigade that he intended to place in the centre of his deployment stronger than the other two brigades; or he might have the cavalry squadrons of the two flanks of his formation in three rather than two lines, or might choose to place squadrons of cavalry as a support behind his first line of infantry battalions.

Of the three Dutch battle formations, the most commonly used before the late 1630s was a model that deployed each of three brigades as a diamond, with infantry battalions forming the points of the diamond; the battalions of each brigade were thus divided between three lines of battle. (A Danish example using this model is illustrated on Plate B.) The distance between the first and second lines should be sufficient for a battalion in the second line to maneuver by wheeling to the right or left. The distance between the second and third lines should be twice the distance between the first and second. The diamond-pattern brigades ensured that the battalions in the second line covered the spaces between those in the first.

The second pattern deployed the infantry to form a flattened wedge formation. This formation was created by deploying all the infantry units in a single line, then advancing central units to form a wedge facing the enemy.

Dutch formation, as demonstrated in front of the Dutch Stadtholder and the visiting Queen of England, Henrietta Maria, at a parade on 4 June 1642. (1) shows the units drawn up in a single line for the initial parade; in (2) the three infantry brigades are drawn up in three separate battle lines.

Israel ex. Cum Privilegio Regis

Recruitment of infantry during the Thirty Years' War. Most of the soldiers who fought in these wars enlisted for pay; the English and the Swedish were exceptional in levying – conscripting – soldiers. Detail from an engraving by Jacques Callot in the series *Les Miseres et les Malheurs de la Guerre,* printed in Paris in 1633.

The head of the wedge would provide a fighting formation in two lines, where the second could support the first (as shown in the example illustrated on page 33, lower) and the remaining battalions were held back on each flank.

The third Dutch formation was added to the other two in the late 1630s. This was the closest to the Roman *triplex acies,* and had certainly been discussed for some time between Prince Maurice and his cousins – there is an earlier example in the surviving papers of Johann of Nassau. This pattern consisted of three lines of infantry, with the first two lines drawn up in a chequerboard formation so that the spaces between the battalions in the first line were covered by those in the second. As with the first type of Dutch deployment, the third line was the reserve, and the space between the second and third lines was twice that between the first and second lines. Hexham gave a theoretical example of this formation in the second part of his *Principles of the Art Militarie,* and the edition printed in 1642 included a demonstration parade of the Dutch army in the presence of the English Queen Henrietta Maria; this placed the battalions of each infantry brigade in its own separate line, those of the Vanguard forming the first line, the Battle the second and the Rearguard the third (see page 41, upper).

The cavalry and artillery

In each of the three Dutch styles of deployment, the majority of the cavalry were formed on the flanks of the infantry, as Hexham wrote: 'The Horse Troupes are commonly ordered, the one halfe on the right, the other halfe on the left flanke of the divisions and Battaillons of foote'. Apart from the tactical possibilities that were inherent to the formation itself – the structure that allowed successive lines to support one another – others could be achieved by specific decisions, such as the relative size and strength of different infantry brigades, or the inclusion of cavalry squadrons to support the first infantry line. The advantage of the latter choice was that the retreat of beaten infantry could be covered by their own supporting cavalry, while a successful infantry attack could be exploited by a cavalry pursuit. The tactic was described by Hexham as placing '*Battaillions* of Horse interlaced, and placed betwixt the *intervals*, and distances of the Foote, as the ground and necessity may require. For, if an Enemies Horse should be ranged betweene his *Battaillions* of foote, it is needefull then, that the other side should observe the same forme likewise, and have horse to encounter horse, least they should breake in upon the foote divisions.'

As with the infantry, Dutch cavalry were armed and equipped on the usual Western European model, as pistol-armed heavy *Reiters* with lighter mounted arquebusiers for support. The mounted infantry role of arquebusiers was assumed in the early 17th century by dragoons – essentially mounted infantry armed with short-barrelled muskets. The papers of Prince Maurice's cousin Johann of Nassau from *c.* 1609–10 refer to these soldiers as '*tragons*' or *trachonz oder musqutirer zu perdt* ('dragoons or musketeers on horseback').

Prince Maurice followed the Spanish example in standardizing his artillery with pieces classed by weight of shot as 48-, 24-, 12- and 6-pdrs, the first two for siege warfare and the latter two for battlefield use. The English officer Sir Edward Cecil observed that Maurice demonstrated lighter artillery in 1622, when 'His Exc[ellency] drewe out in Battalia' for a parade deployment at Rozendale near Bergen-op-Zoom, where 'to every Manipall or Battalion there was allowed two of his Exc newe devised peeces called Drakes'. Hexham described four types of drakes, this being a lighter type of artillery with shorter barrels firing 24-pound, 12-pound, 6-pound and 3-pound shot. The drakes which Cecil saw in 1622 were probably the light 3-pdrs – he brought ten of this type back to London in 1625.

THE THIRTY YEARS' WAR

Prince Maurice's publicity for his reforms, spread by reports of his victory at Nieupoort and through a series of public demonstrations and parades, had a strong influence on opinion in Western Europe, particularly in Protestant countries that shared his need to counter the threat of the veteran Spanish army. The dissemination of the new theory and practice was also assisted by the fact that the rebel Dutch army included regiments of Germans, French, English and Scots, and Maurice's training manuals included versions in the languages spoken in the various regiments (the infantry instructions for basic orders in 1597 were recorded in Dutch, German, French, English, Scots and Latin). The Dutch also directly provided training officers to German states including Brandenburg, the Palatinate, Baden, Wurtemberg, Hesse, Brunswick, Saxony and Holstein; and Prince Maurice sent a Dutch captain, Abraham van Nyevelt, to assist in the military education of the then-heir to the English throne, King James I's short-lived eldest son Henry Stuart. Dutch influence extended as far as Switzerland, where in 1615 the Republic of Berne published instructions on arms-handling and basic drill for its militia based on the Dutch model, as *Brief Recueil de Milice … conforme a celoy de tres illustre & Tres haut Prince, Maurice Prince d'Orange.*

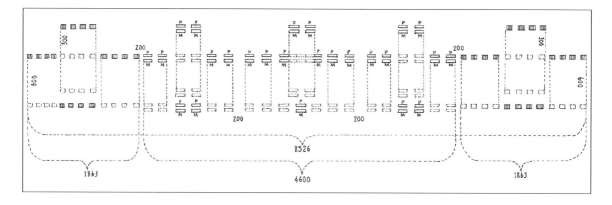

ABOVE AND OPPOSITE
Two Danish battle plans,
July 1625; see also Plate B.
The army of King Christian IV
of Denmark, which took part in
the Thirty Years' War between
1625 and 1629, was strongly
influenced by Dutch theories,
and these two formations are
clearly modelled on the Dutch
diamond-pattern brigade and
wedge-shaped battle line.

The ideas behind Prince Maurice's reforms had been strongly influenced by his cousin Prince Johann, whose reputation extended well outside the United Provinces. Notable examples of Johann's influence (and that of his son-in-law, the Landgraf Moritz von Hessen) amongst military commentators were Wilhelm Dillich and Johann Jacobi von Walhausen. Dillich's *Kriegsbuch* was published in Kassel in 1607, and Walhausen produced a series of works on the art of war between 1615 and 1621.[3] Walhausen was also involved with Prince Johann in setting up a military academy – the *Ritterliche Kriegschule* – at Siegen in 1616, and became its director. The curriculum included 'the handling of weapons, including the pike, drill in the Dutch style', marching and battle formations, their variation under battle conditions, and the besieging and defence of fortifications.

In France, the influence of new Dutch theories can be seen in texts from a group of predominantly Protestant authors. After meeting Prince Maurice in 1600, in 1603 Louis de Montgomery, Sieur de Courbouzon devoted a chapter in his book on tactics to the 'evolutions and exercises that are used in the Dutch army'. Both Jean de Billon – author of *Les Principes de l'Art Militaire* (Paris, 1612) and *Instructions Militaires* (Lyon, 1617) – and Henri, Duc de Rohan, whose *The Parfaict Capitaine* was published in Paris in 1636, had served with the Dutch army. The background of the Sieur du Praissac, whose *Discours Militaires* was published in Paris in 1612, is not known, but his work refers directly to Prince Maurice's campaigns; it illustrates two versions of the Dutch practice deployments on their march to Julich in 1610, and the illustrations of arms drill are based on Jacob de Gheyn's weapons-handling manual. Language was no barrier to the dissemination of these ideas; Walhausen's works on infantry and cavalry were printed in German and French when first published, and were frequently reprinted in both languages. Walhausen himself translated Billon's *Instructions Militaires* into German; Praissac's *Discours Militaires* was translated into German in Frankfurt in 1616, into Dutch in Amsterdam in 1627, and into English in Cambridge in 1639.

French officers also served in Catholic armies; some in the Spanish Army of Flanders would have fought against their fellow countrymen serving in the Dutch army, and by the late 1620s there are clear indications of Dutch

---

3 *Kriegskunst zu Fuss* (Openheim, 1615); *Kriegskunst zu Pferd* (Frankfurt, 1616); the arms-drill manuals *Alphabetum pro tyrone pedestri* (Frankfurt, 1615) and *Kunstlichen Piquen-Handling* (Hanau, 1617); and *Defensio Patriae oder Landrettung* (Frankfurt, 1621), *Landrettung* being the idea of a local militia trained on Dutch lines.

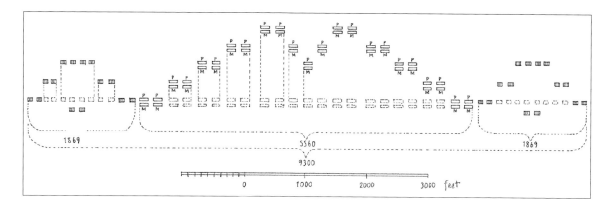

influence on French deployments. The detail of a French deployment during the siege of La Rochelle by Jacques Callot (illustrated on page 38) shows two diamond-pattern formations on the Dutch model. Cardinal Richelieu's description of the deployment of the French army at Casale in 1630 also shows clear similarities with Dutch practice.

Although Spanish military literature shows a knowledge of Maurice's reforms, the Spanish saw few battlefield examples of the new Dutch style and retained confidence in the value of large individual formations. An example is the *Discourse of Militarie Discipline* by the Irish officer Gerat Barry, which was published in Brussels in 1634. Barry had spent 'thirty-three yeares in this my present profession of armes, in his Catholicke Majesties service amongst the Spaniard, Italian and Irish,' including '29 yeares in the warres, and brave expolites in the lowe countries, and Germany'. Barry's book has elements of earlier works, but provides a useful indication that Spanish military theory and practice retained its trust in large formations, while considering the value of smaller units. There are also indications of developments in Spanish thinking about infantry firing systems, as Barry also describes a form of firing while retreating as 'retiring backe upon a countermarche each feele [file] or ranke, consequently'; the use of the word 'countermarch' is a clear echo of one of Prince Maurice's Dutch firing systems.

Battle plan for a German Imperialist army, 1632. The Swedish victory at Breitenfeld the previous year shattered Count Tilly's army, and his replacement, Albrecht von Wallenstein, introduced a different tactical model for the 1632 campaign. This re-drawn copy has the same unit symbols as in the original. Note the chequerboard deployment of infantry units, and supporting cavalry behind the first and third lines.

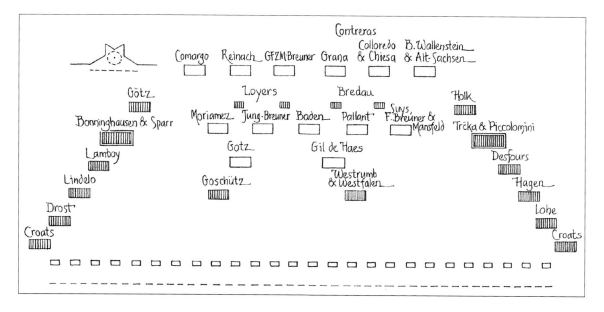

The early campaigns

The deployment style of Protestant armies at the outbreak of the Thirty Years' War in 1618 was certainly influenced by Dutch theories. Contemporary plans of deployments of the Danish army in 1625 (see pages 44–45) are close copies of the Dutch diamond- and wedge-pattern deployments. Danish infantry and cavalry were equipped in the same manner as the Dutch, and Danish artillery was standardized by King Christian IV on five calibres – 48-, 24-, 12-, 6- and 3-pdrs, the latter three being field pieces.

Nevertheless, the armies of the German Protestant commanders and of the Danes suffered a series of defeats by opponents whose military thinking followed Spanish and Catholic German models rather than Dutch. King Christian IV ended his support of the Protestant cause in Germany at the Peace of Lubeck in 1629, and disbanded the majority of his army. Officers and soldiers from the Danish army – some of whom had served with the Protestant general Ernst, Count Mansfeld's army before joining Danish service – now joined the army of Gustavus Adolphus of Sweden, as he recruited men during 1629–30 in preparation for a landing in Germany. In some cases entire regiments – such as Mac-Keys (Mackay's) Scottish infantry regiment, and two complete German arquebusier cavalry regiments – were recruited from the Danish to the Swedish service.

THE SWEDISH INTERVENTION

The reforms of the Swedish army under King Gustavus Adolphus were shaped both by his wars with Poland, whose cavalry were superior, and by the debate around military ideas current in the United Provinces and, with variations, throughout northern Europe – particularly through the published works of Walhausen. Gustavus Adolphus was studying military theory at the time when Walhausen's books were appearing, and during his tour of Germany in 1620 he met Prince Maurice's cousin Johann of Nassau. This military debate took place during the period following the first impact of Maurice's reforms, at a time when further options arising out of these were

 SPANISH AND FRENCH FORMATIONS AT ROCROI, 1643

This illustration is also based on a contemporary engraving from *Theatrum Europaeum;* it was copied as part of the later engraving by the engineer officer Sebastien de Pontault, Sieur de Beaulieu, who was present at the battle on 19 May 1643. The Spanish army **(top)** was commanded by Don Francisco de Melo, and the French army **(bottom)** by the 22-year-old Louis, Duc d'Enghien, better known by his future title of Prince de Condé – who won a decisive victory at Rocroi.

Spanish veteran *tercios* probably retained deep formations, but their deployment showed that the Spanish army had now adopted the German style which evolved during the Thirty Years' War as a composite of the Dutch and Swedish doctrines. The Spanish army, both infantry centre and cavalry wings, are deployed in two-line chequerboard; the only cavalry support for the infantry centre is a small reserve placed behind the second line. A body of commanded musketeers (not shown)

was placed in the wood on the left of the line, but there are none deployed in support of the cavalry wings.

The French army also shows a composite German-style deployment but in a far more sophisticated variation, using three lines of infantry with the battalions in the third, reserve line alternating with cavalry squadrons (including heavy armoured *gensdarmes*). Bodies of commanded musketeers are deployed in the Swedish style, here in front of the cavalry squadrons in the first line on each wing (**m & c**).

This plate reproduces the spacings between units as shown in the original engraving. This may accurately represent a decision by each side to reduce the intervals in response to the ground over which they deployed; however, it may also be the result of a common convention amongst engravers to reduce the intervals in order to make a more dramatically compact image.

Inset 1: French *carabins* cavalry, in five ranks.

Inset 2: Croat irregular cavalry in Imperial/Spanish service, drawn up in loose ranks.

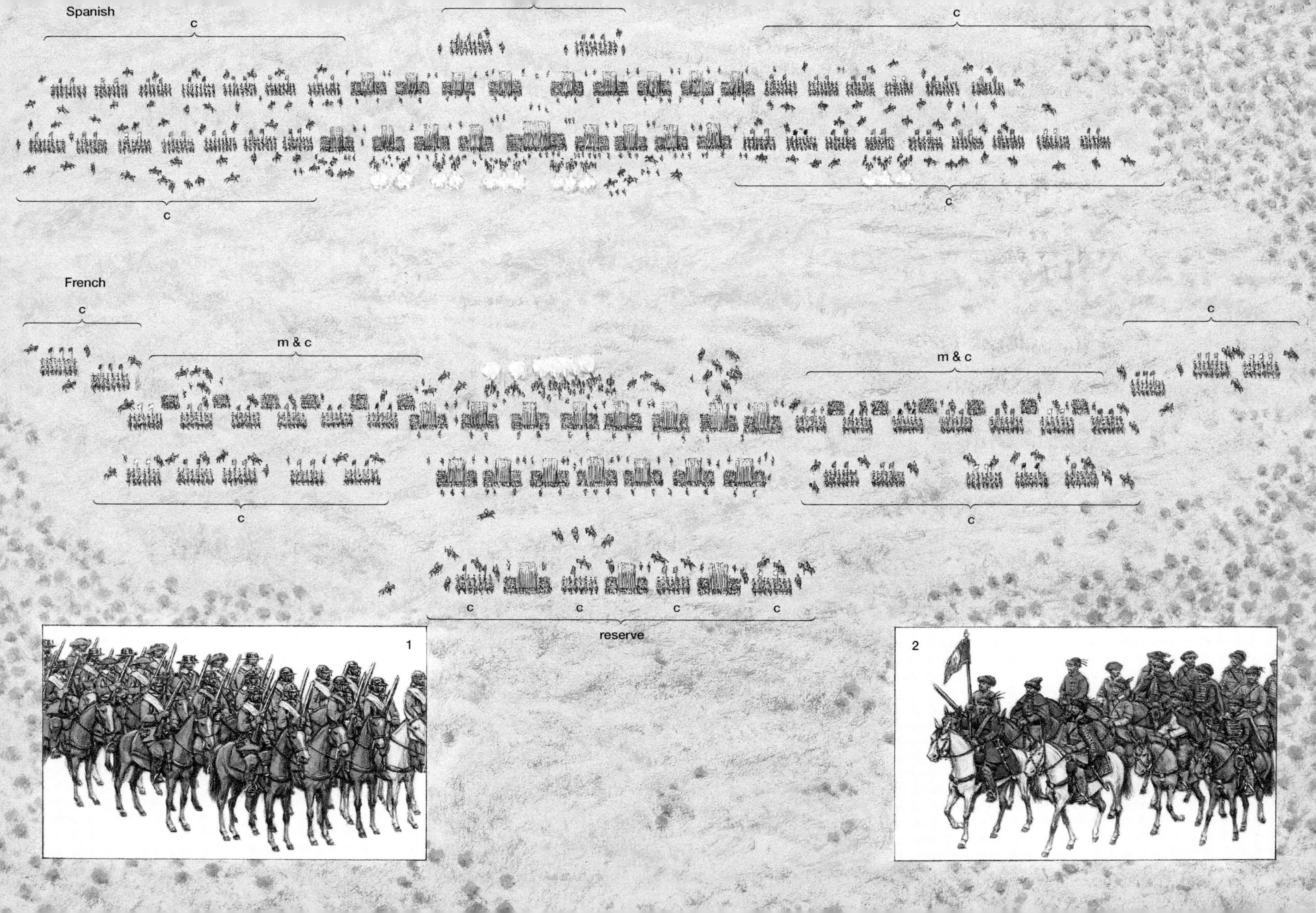

Spanish

French

m & c

m & c

c

c

c

c

c

c

c

c

c

c

c

c

c

c

reserve

1

2

Swedish/North German musketeer and pikeman on the frontispiece of Laurentius à Troupitzen's *Kriegs Kunst nach Koniglicher Schwedischer Manier* … ('The Art of War in the Royal Swedish Style') published in Frankfurt in 1633. This is a training manual for a company, not a battalion or a brigade, and its content is similar to a Dutch company manual. (By permission The British Library)

being considered. Gustavus' Polish experience had taught him that since he had inferior cavalry he had to factor in ways of providing infantry firepower support for them, as well as infantry formations with the capability to survive cavalry attack without being immobilized.

The theoretical model for Swedish infantry was set in 1621 as a regiment of eight companies, each of 16 officers and non-commissioned officers and 126 corporals and men – 54 pikemen and 72 musketeers. A regiment would thus consist of 1,008 men, the same number as the theoretical Dutch regiment described by Henry Hexham. As with the Dutch battalions, a Swedish regiment would be divided to form two units (called 'squadrons' in Swedish usage), each of about 500 rankers plus NCOs and officers. The Swedish 'squadron', like the Dutch 'battalion' of similar size, was formed from groups of files into sub-units armed alike, although the Swedish system used a higher number of corporals – six in the Swedish company, rather than three in the Dutch. The depth of the file was reduced from the ten of the Dutch file to six men. In the Swedish system, each of the six sub-units equivalent to the Dutch 'divisions' – three of pikemen (each of three *rots* or files) and three of musketeers (each of four rots) – had its own corporal, and these sub-units were called 'corporalships'. One of the three musketeer corporalships from any company could be withdrawn for special duties, including supporting the cavalry wings or forming a 'Forlorn Hope' ahead of the army.

As with the Dutch regiment or the large Spanish formations, the Swedish object was to form their soldiers into their general's preferred fighting units. The Swedish battlefield formation – the Swedish brigade – was formed of squadrons, each squadron theoretically composed of four full-strength companies or more if they were weak. (In practice the regiments of the Swedish army, whether raised in Sweden or from foreign mercenaries, had different numbers of companies, and campaign conditions reduced the number of men per company.) This was a flexible system, as the English officer William Barriffe commented: 'By the standing of this Squadron, or third part of a Brigade, you may easily perceive how apt and ready they are to be imbattelled into any form, either offensive or defensive'.

The Swedish brigades themselves were formed of either three squadrons to form an arrowhead formation, or four squadrons to form a diamond; the three-squadron version was the more commonly used, the four-squadron brigade (see Plate C) being employed only briefly between 1628 and 1631. Like the Dutch, the Swedish brigade was designed to be flexible, and in this respect the structure of these formations surpassed the Dutch. On the practical realities of composition, Barriffe commented that 'one regiment and a half, of whole and full companies, would perfect a Brigade: or two regiments of torne and broken companies, the overplus being always added to the Reserve. Notwithstanding it so happened at the Battell of Lutzen, that Miezlaff, Gerstorfs, and Rosses, 3. crazed [broken] Regiments made up but one Brigade, being the outmost Brigade to the left of the second Range. And towards night in the same forenamed Battell, going to rally up the two broken and shattered brigades of yellow and blew, belonging to Grave Neeles, and Colonel Winkle, there were not men enough left unhurt and killed, wherewith to make one Squadron.'

Firing systems

Swedish musketeers could be drawn up for firing in corporalships (4 rots) or *plottons* (8 rots). They were trained to fire both in the Dutch style and in the distinctive Swedish 'salvee' or volley.

The Swedish variation of the Dutch style was to fire rank by rank, but while the Dutch musketeers fired and retired one rank at a time the Swedes fired two ranks together. The Scottish officer Robert Munro wrote that the Swedish salvee was 'ordinarie in Battell, before an enemy joyne, or against Horsemen', and it was achieved by three ranks firing together in one volley. There were two methods to achieve this. The first was by bringing forward the rear three ranks – the rear half of the six-deep formation – alongside the front three. The officer was to 'command the bringers up or Reare to double the Front to the right hand [i.e. the rear three ranks of each file to march up on the right alongside the front three ranks], and to make readie, having the match cocked and their panes [priming pans] well guarded, having closed the three Rancks but not the Files, the Officers standing in equall Front with the Foremost Rancke, betwixt two Divisions, he commands to give fire'. A contemporary description of Swedish musketeers at Breitenfeld records the way three ranks could fire together as 'the first ranck falling upon their knees, the second

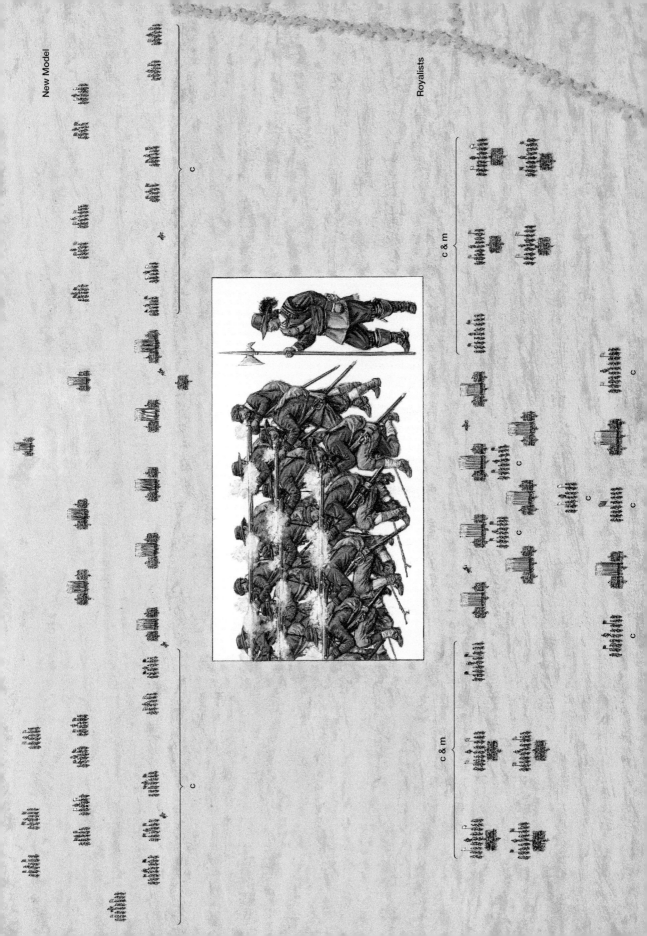

New Model

Royalists

c

c & m

c & m

c

c

c

c

c

c

stooping forward, and the third standing upright and all giving fire together'. The second method was to fire the first three ranks in volley, then march the rear three ranks forwards in front of the first and fire a second volley.

Cavalry and artillery

The theoretical model for Swedish cavalry in 1621 was the Dutch arquebusier, but without the arquebus. The Swedish also hired German mercenary cavalry, some cuirassiers but mostly arquebusiers, and German arquebusiers probably retained their carbines. As with the lighter-armed Huguenot cavalry in the late 16th century, circumstances obliged the Swedish to use light horse as battle cavalry rather than simply in support. Count Tilly, who commanded the Imperial army at the battle of Breitenfeld in 1631, had been recorded as saying that 'he never seriously considered the using arquebusiers in a military engagement', so the Swedish cavalry must have come as an unpleasant surprise. Certainly Tilly underestimated them, as he did the rest of the Swedish army that day. By 1632 Swedish cavalry were drawn up three deep rather than the five-deep of the Dutch army. Gustavus Adolphus' instructions for their attack were that 'only the first or at most the first two ranks, when near enough, to see the whites of the enemy's eyes, were to give fire, then to reach for their swords; the last rank however was to attack without shooting but with swords drawn, and to keep both pistols (or in the front ranks, one) for the mêlée'.

As with the Spanish and the Dutch, Gustavus' reforms standardized artillery calibres, but he went further, reducing the number to three and employing only the 24-pdrs for siege work and the 12- and 3-pdrs for field artillery. The use of light 3-pdr guns was not new, as the Dutch already used 3-pdr drakes, but the overall weight of the gun was reduced to make it more mobile and capable of keeping pace with advancing infantry.

SWEDISH BRIGADE DEPLOYMENT

The Swedish battle formation used its brigades as individual tactical units, and drew them up one alongside another in two lines of infantry brigades. At Breitenfeld (1631) there were seven infantry brigades, with four in the first

---

G ENGLISH ROYALIST AND PARLIAMENTARIAN FORMATIONS AT NASEBY, 1645

This plate is based on a manuscript representation of the Royalist formation by Sir Bernard de Gomme. There are two detailed contemporary illustrations of this battle, the other being an engraving by Robert Streeter which was published bound with Joshua Sprigge's *Anglia Rediviva* in 1647. De Gomme's plan shows the optimum spacings between units, while Streeter's engraving reduces them.

As the Royalist formation at Edgehill in 1642 showed Swedish influence, so that at Naseby on 14 June 1645 (**bottom**) shows the influence of the Duc d'Enghien's deployment at Rocroi (see Plate F). Since the Parliament armies refused to fight Prince Rupert during his relief of Donnington Castle in October 1644, Naseby was Rupert's first opportunity to use this formation in practice. He deployed three lines of infantry with similar spacing between the lines to d'Enghien's, the third or

reserve line being composed of alternating infantry and cavalry units. Prince Rupert placed supporting cavalry squadrons behind both the first and second infantry lines, and deployed commanded musketeers to support the squadrons in both of his two lines of cavalry – (**c & m**).

The opposing formation of the Parliament's New Model Army (**top**) commanded by Sir Thomas Fairfax was much simpler, with two lines of infantry, and the only infantry reserve was a single battalion formed from half a regiment. The cavalry were formed in two lines on the army's left flank and three lines on the stronger right, commanded by Oliver Cromwell. No supporting cavalry were deployed behind the infantry lines or commanded musketeers among the cavalry wings. The New Model Army won a decisive victory at Naseby.

Inset: New Model Army musketeers drawn up for firing in the Swedish three-rank style.

line and three in the second; at Lützen the following year there were eight brigades, four in each line (see page 54). The formation was based on the Dutch diamond-pattern wedge, but was significantly different from the original models. Dutch infantry deployments relied on the integrity of the formation as a whole, and could be used flexibly to sustain it by bringing forward successive lines. The Swedish brigades were designed to fight temporarily as separate entities, making them more resistant to cavalry attack.

Soldiers who were already experienced in Dutch and Danish tactics could quickly be re-trained in the basics of the Swedish practice, since the drills were the same. However, the Swedish tactical formation was more complex than the Dutch, and only veteran soldiers could achieve competence in it quickly. Robert Munro recorded that at a parade in Sweden in 1630, Gustavus Adolphus commended McKay's Regiment, which had recently transferred from the Danish army to the Swedish, on their ability to deploy 'after his new order of Discipline of Briggads', and said that he wished 'all his Foot were so well disciplined' [well trained, in this context].

Munro's account of the Swedish army at Breitenfeld provides a good example of the Swedish army in operation. The Swedes and their Saxon allies formed up side by side but as two separate armies, with each using its own form of deployment; the Saxons used a version of the Dutch wedge formation, while the Swedes deployed in their distinctive brigades. Munro described the Swedish army drawing up in battle formation and then marching forward to the battlefield, which was consistent with Dutch practice. On the battlefield itself, Gustavus Adolphus personally checked the positions of his infantry and cavalry.

The Swedes deployed supporting cavalry squadrons behind both the first and second lines of infantry, as distinct from the Dutch practice which placed them behind the first line only. The cavalry wings were reinforced with 'commanded musketeers' – a Swedish innovation that differed from Dutch practice. At Lützen in 1632 the Swedes added light artillery to support their cavalry wings as well as commanded musketeers. The reason for this tactic is likely to be that the fact that the Swedish battle cavalry wore less armour and were at a disadvantage against the opposing cuirassiers, so needed the extra fire support.

The lines of Swedish infantry brigades at Breitenfeld were drawn up in a chequerboard pattern. Barriffe described this as 'the usuall & accustomed manner of Imbattelling by that invinceable King of Sweden, of never dying memory; who placed them as in this Figure may be seen. The Battell of the following Brigade [i.e. the brigade in the second line] being always placed directly behind the Intervall Division, or space of ground between the two wings of the former Brigades' [this means that the distance between two brigades in the front line was the frontage of the pike without their musketeer wings in the second line]. Munro described how 'the whole Armie: both the Dukes, and Ours were put in good order; our Armie marching on the right hand, and the Dukes on the left, our commanded Musketeres marching in the Van-Guarde, being in one bodie before the Armie …. We marched thus, both the Armies in Battaile, Horse, Foote, and Artillerie, till about nine of the Clocke in the morning'.

On the deployment itself, Munro wrote that Gustavus Adolphus 'appointed Plottons of musketiers by fifties [a plotton was formed of two corporalships, so comprised eight files each of six men, 48 musketeers in all], which were commanded by sufficient Officers to attend on severall regiments of horse …

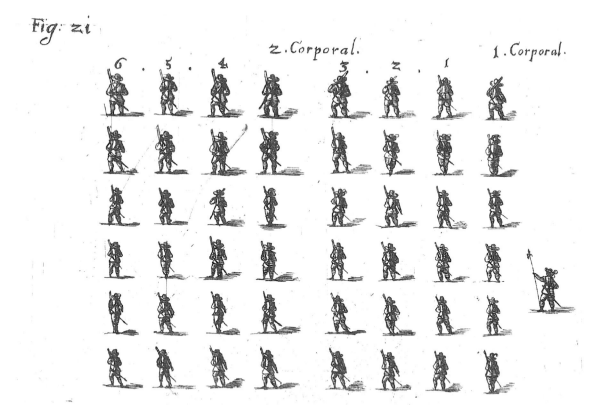

Fig: 21

6 . 5 . 4   2. Corporal.   3 . 2 . 1   1. Corporal.

which orderly done, the commanded Musketiers were directed to their stand where to fight; his Majestie then led up the foure Briggads of Foote, which were appointed to be the Battaile of the Armie [first line of infantry units], with a distance between each Briggad, that a Regiment of horse might march out in grosse betwixt the Briggads, all four being in one Front, having their Ordnance [artillery] planted before every Briggad.'

For the second infantry line, 'Behinde these foure Briggads were drawne up the three Briggads of Reserve with their artillery before them standing at a proportionable distance behinde the other four Briggads, with like distance betwixt them, as was betwixt the Briggads of the Battaile. The Briggads of Horse which had Plottons of Musketiers to attend them were placed on the right and left wings of the foote, and some were placed betwixt the Battaile of foote and the Reserve, to second the foote as neede were: other Briggads of horse were drawne up behinde the Reserve of foote Briggads'.

The Swedish army in battle

In his account of the battle itself Munro describes the advance of pike and shot together, as 'our small Ordinance [light artillery] being twice discharged amongst them, and before we stirred, we charged them with a salvee of muskets, which was repaied, and incontinent our Briggad advancing unto them with push of pike, putting one of their battailes in disorder, fell on the execution, so that they were put to the route'. In describing the cavalry action, Munro wrote that:

By halfe three, our Cannon a little ceasing, the Horsemen on both wings charged furiously one another, our Horsemen with a resolution, abiding

A 'plotton' of two musketeer 'divisions' or 'corporalships' side by side, totalling 48 men, from Troupitzen's Swedish company manual. Each corporalship comprises four files of six men, the right-hand file led by the corporal. Note the sergeant, identified by his halberd, outside the ranks to the right. (By permission The British Library)

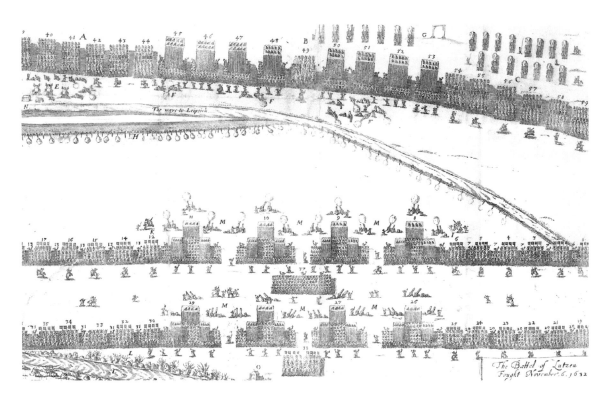

The Battel of Lutzen
Fought November 6, 1632

Battle of Lützen, 6 November 1632, in an engraving from the English newsbook *The Swedish Intelligencer*. This shows only the front line of the Imperialist army (top); but note the characteristic appearance of the Swedish brigades in the foreground – compare with Plates C & D. (By permission The British Library)

unloosing a Pistoll, till the enemy had discharged first, and then at a neere distance our Musketiers meeting them with a Salve; then our horsemen discharged their Pistolls, and then charged through them with swords; and at theire returne the Musketiers were ready againe to give the second Salve of Musket amongst them: the enemy thus valiantly resisted by our Horsemen, and cruelly plagued by our plottons of Musketiers: you may imagine, howe soone he would be discouraged from charging twice in this manner, and repulsed.

The advantage of the Swedish brigade system for 'all-round defence' was famously demonstrated at this battle, since the Imperial army broke the Saxon formation that formed the left of the allied army, but failed to make headway against the Swedish on the right. The second line of Swedish brigades then wheeled to their left and fell upon the Imperial infantry, which was probably reforming after scattering the Saxons. To move an entire second infantry line across the battlefield was highly unusual, and the Swedish brigade structure – where each brigade formed part of the line but could operate with some independence – made it far easier to carry out that would have been possible with the Dutch linear formations, which were far more dependent on the units on either side of them.

William Watts' account of the Swedish victory at Breitenfeld referred to the value of smaller, more flexible tactical units in the same terms as Henry Hexham had used to describe Prince Maurice's victory at Nieupoort. He described the Swedish as using 'a new kind of marshalling was this unto Tilly, which as much helped to beate him, as the valoour of the men did, that fought in it. Every part of it consisted of several Maniples and small bodyes of men; of which if any one were overthrowne, there was nothing so much hurt done, as when one of Tilly's greater battaglons were broken'

The Imperial response

Imperial and Catholic League armies had also been influenced by the changes introduced into the Dutch army, and the military literature and experiments in Germany and Denmark that had followed it. The influential *De Militia Equestri* by Hermann Hugo, published in Antwerp in 1630 and dedicated to King Philip IV of Spain, drew on developing Spanish and Imperial theories as well as those of northern Europe. It referred to both the Italian Ludovico Melzo's *Regole Militari sopra il governo e servitio particulare della cavelleria*, and the dragoon and cavalry formations from the Protestant German Johann Jacobi von Walhausen's *Kriegskunst zu Pferd*. Imperial commanders had begun to make changes in the size and depth of their infantry formations, and to introduce lighter regimental artillery.

The defeat at Breitenfeld was catastrophic in terms both of casualties among veteran soldiers and of the reputation of Imperial arms, and accelerated the rate of change. Under its new commander, Albrecht von Wallenstein, the Imperial army drawn up at the battle of Lützen in 1632 adopted a field deployment of three lines of infantry battalions. The battalions (sometimes termed 'brigades') had around 1,000 men drawn up with a reduced depth; Monteccuoli referred to a file of seven men for the pike block in 1632 (when the horse included both full cuirassiers and lighter-armed battle cavalry). This formation, influenced by the Dutch but also using the Swedish model of forming small infantry brigades as fighting units rather than simply a deployment tool, was the foundation of the composite German style. The Swedish brigade formation itself did not long survive its creator, and defeat at Nordlingen in 1634 forced change on the Swedish army. By the later 1630s, armies on both sides were using versions of the composite German tactical style.

Three Swedish brigades in two lines, that in the second covering the gap between the two in the first line. Under magnification, the annotations on this illustration – from William Barriffe's *Military Discipline or the Young Artilleryman* – identify each of the three oblong blocks with flags in a brigade as 36 *rotts* or six-man files of pike (216 men), and each of its six small squares as a *plotton* of eight *rotts* of musketeers (48 men). Here, two of these *plottons* of shot are detached from each of a brigade's three 'squadrons' (battalions) and are lined up in the rear, but they might well be sent further away to provide fire support for the cavalry wings as 'commanded musketeers'. Note that the interval between the two front-line brigades is the same as the frontage of the front pike block of the brigade behind them.

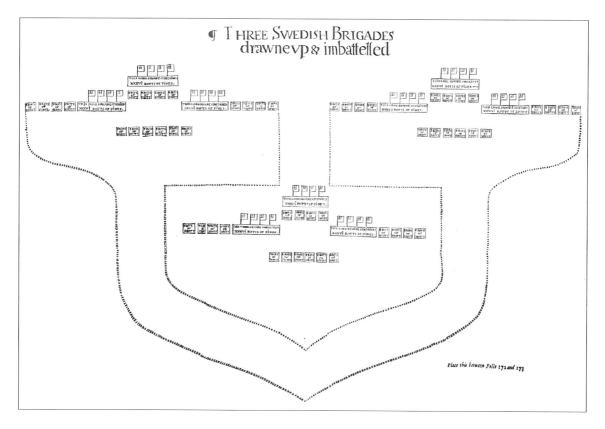

THE ENGLISH CIVIL WARS

Most Englishmen with any professional experience before 1642 had served in the Dutch army, and the English militia at home was trained using an English-language version of Dutch manuals. However, although military thinking was solidly based on the Dutch model, professional officers and other Englishmen with an interest in military affairs – typically gentlemen, officers in the militia and members of the urban voluntary companies – were influenced to varying extents by the Swedish and German styles of which they had read or been told by friends.

Engravings of the English army during the Bishops' Wars of 1639–40 show a demonstration deployment clearly based on the classic Dutch diamond pattern, but this does not mean that Englishmen with a background in either professional service abroad or the Trained Bands in England were ignorant of the changes arising from the Thirty Years' War. George Monk's comments in his *Observations on Military and Political Affairs* (*c.* 1646) provide an example of a professional officer who had served in the Dutch army but whose ideas were influenced by Swedish practices; he recommended infantry files six deep, and the use of a version of the Swedish salvee. Books by William Barriffe (*Military Discipline, or the Young Artilleryman*) and Robert Elton (*The Compleat Body of the Art Militarie*) provide examples of the views of influential militia officers, both of whom later fought in the Civil Wars; and

English deployment in the Dutch diamond pattern, 1639. The core of professional officers who served in these Bishops' Wars against Scotland had obtained their military experience during service in the Dutch army.

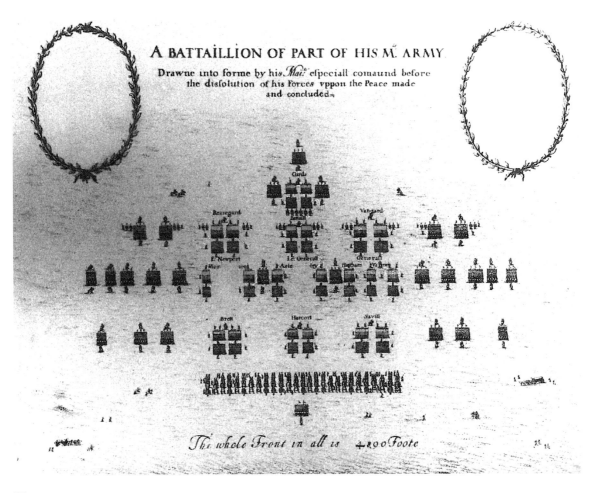

A BATTAILLION OF PART OF HIS M. ARMY.
Drawne into forme by his Mai: especiall comaund before the dissolution of his Forces vppon the Peace made and concluded.

The whole Front in all is 4290 Foote

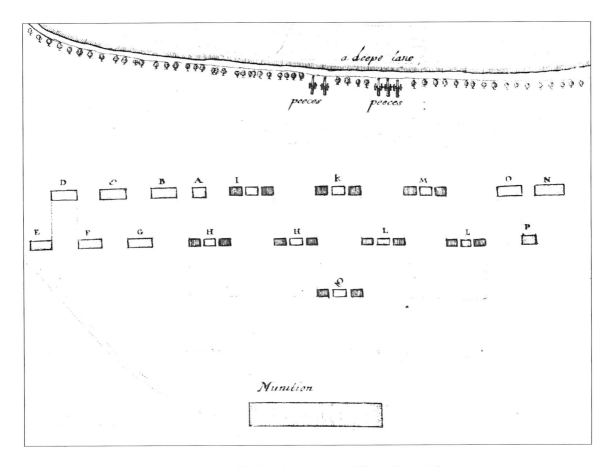

a deepe lane

peeces   peeces

D   C   B   A   I   k   M   O   N

E   F   G   H   H   L   L   P

Munition

Swedish practice was also disseminated by books such as William Watts' *The Swedish Discipline* and Col Robert Munro's *Monro His Expedition with the Worthy Scots Regiment (called Mac-Keyes)*.

Many English professional officers who had returned to serve in King Charles I's army in the Bishops' Wars went on to serve during the Irish Revolt in the regiments raised in England or amongst English settlers in Ireland. A key indication of the impact of changing military ideas is an engraving by Wenceslaus Hollar (see above) of an English army deployed for battle in Ireland in 1642 – one of the English officers present was George Monk. This is the closest contemporary illustration of English military practice to the outbreak of the Civil War later that year, and shows the deployment of a small English army with around 2,400 infantry. The Earl of Ormonde, who commanded it, employed the same principles of deployment as he would have used for a main field army. He needed to retain the flexibility of the battle formations in which his men had been trained to fight, but to achieve this with so few men he reduced the number of soldiers in his battalions to around 300 in each, dividing each of his two largest regiments into two battalions which would fight as separate units. He also deployed his 400-odd cavalry into troop-sized bodies of around 30 troopers each.

This army was on the march in enemy territory when Ormonde's 'scouts came in, and brought in intelligence'. He then brought forward and deployed his leading units according to his chosen campaign plan, making a 'stand with the first four divisions of Foot, drew them up in order to Fight … leaving room for the other Troops of Horse and Foot according to the ground, and

English deployment in Ireland, 1642. This detail from an engraving by Wenceslaus Hollar shows an English army in a more modern deployment of two lines, with cavalry units on the flanks, and a single infantry unit in reserve. (In this plan, confusingly, the engraver changed the notation: here a single block indicates cavalry, and three side-by-side an infantry unit.) After the Bishops' Wars many unemployed professional officers joined the English regiments sent to Ireland. (By permission The British Library)

Deployments and frontages: both examples show the deployment of infantry in chequerboard pattern with units in one line covering gaps in the other. This was achieved by forming units up in a single line, and then moving some out to form a second.

(1) Deployment as described by Roger Boyle, Earl of Orrery, in his *A Treatise of the Art of War* (London, 1677).

(2) & (3) Deployment of London Militia, Trained Bands and Auxiliaries at a parade in Hyde Park on 23 May 1644, described and illustrated in a contemporary pamphlet *Orders to be observed in the Marching, Imbatelling, Fighting and Dismarching of the Citie Forces.* In (2), units 1 to 8 are Trained Band regiments and 9 to 12 are Auxiliary regiments. For this parade, six regiments were drawn up facing the other six.

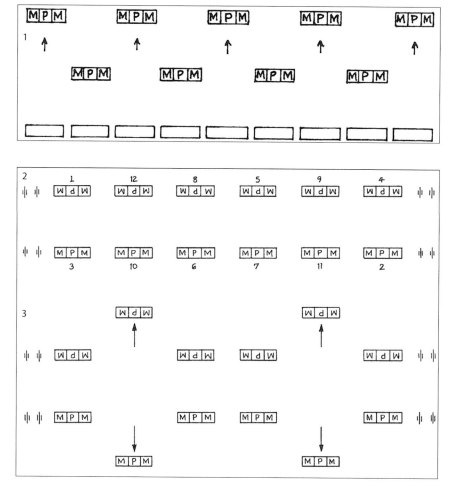

the order he had designed to draw them up in,' while the second infantry brigade came up behind. This army was drawn up in two lines and, despite its small size, a single battalion of 300 men was held back as a final reserve. At the battle of Naseby in 1645 the much larger New Model Army used a similar infantry deployment, with two infantry lines and half a regiment held back as a final reserve behind them (see Plate G).

H   CAVALRY DEPLOYMENT

These illustrations show two tactical elements of cavalry deployment.

1: The first is the tactic of attaching *plottons* of musketeers in support of the cavalry on the wings of an army. In the approach these 'commanded musketeers' march behind the cavalry, but in action they are deployed alongside the cavalry squadrons.

2a & 2b: The second shows the differences between the chequerboard pattern of deploying cavalry squadrons – where the squadrons in the second line cover gaps between squadrons in the first – and an alternative, where the second-line squadrons are placed immediately behind the front-line squadrons. The logic was that whereas a routed infantry unit can run straight backwards, a routed cavalry unit wheels round to a flank; if the two lines are drawn up chequerboard-fashion then the routed cavalry will ride into their supports. If the second-line units are directly behind the first line, then the fleeing troopers from the front line will avoid their supports. The Imperialist commander Raimondo Monteccuoli described this tactic when writing in c. 1642. Some 17th-century commanders followed this logic, others disagreed; Prince Rupert, who had met Imperialist officers, used it for his deployment at Donnington Castle and at the battle of Naseby.

3: The right flank of a New Model Army cavalry unit in three-rank formation; the cornet rides at the right end of the front rank, with the commander and his trumpeter slightly out to the flank.

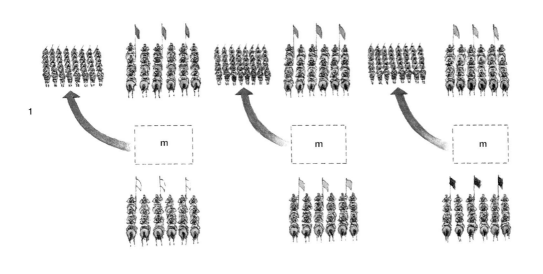

1

2a

2b

3

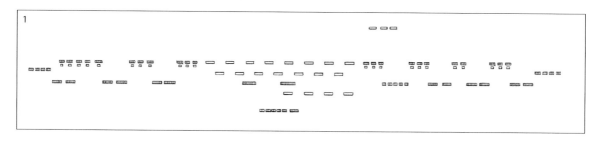

(1) Royalist deployment at Marston Moor, 2 July 1644, based on the plan drawn by Sir Bernard de Gomme. The plan shows three lines of infantry, cavalry squadrons in direct support of the infantry centre, and the Swedish tactic of placing 'commanded musketeer' *plottons* to support the cavalry wings.

(2) Part of the deployment of the allied Parliament and Scots armies at Marston Moor, from De Gomme's plan. Note the infantry brigades each formed in two bodies.

(3) Fragment of the plan by the Scots Sergeant-Major General, James Lumsden. Note the placing of musketeer detachments (flagged) among the cavalry; Lumsden had served in the Swedish army. The shading for cavalry units is incomplete in this paper; only the blank oblongs in the centre represent infantry bodies of both pike and shot.

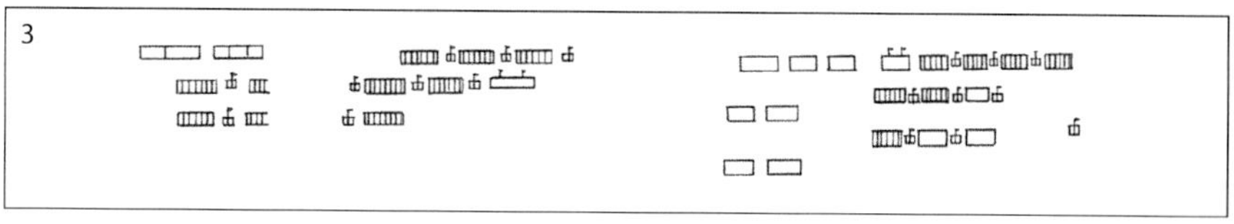

```
3
```
(Plan fragment illustration with numbered panel "3")

Prince Rupert at Edgehill, 1642

At the outbreak of the English Civil Wars both armies, Royalist and Parliamentarian, were initially trained on the Dutch model, and indeed the two commanding generals – Robert Bertie, Earl of Lindsey for the Royalists, and Robert Devereux, Earl of Essex for the Parliament – had served together as colonels in the Dutch army. However, Lindsey gave up his command after a series of quarrels with King Charles' nephew, Prince Rupert. Prince Rupert had limited practical experience but an unusually broad exposure to theory, since he grew up in exile in Holland, served briefly in Germany, and met Habsburg officers while he was a prisoner of war. His chaplain in England was the same Dr William Watts who had written both *The Swedish Discipline*, and a series of newsbooks published as *The Swedish Intelligencer* which described the Swedish campaigns in Germany.

Like many young officers who sought a quick military reputation, Prince Rupert was inspired by the aggressive tactical approach and decisive victories of Gustavus Adolphus, and through his influence the Royalist army was deployed at Edgehill – the first battle of the Civil War – with its infantry in the Swedish brigade pattern, and both cavalry and infantry in the Swedish unit depths of six-deep and three-deep respectively. The Royalist battle plan survives as a more carefully drawn copy by one of Prince Rupert's staff officers, Sir Bernard de Gomme, and it shows five Royalist infantry brigades in two lines, each brigade in the Swedish 'four-squadron' formation. The model he used was probably that described by Lord Rhees and illustrated by Dr Watts. While this was certainly an effective tactical style, it was more complicated to operate than either the Dutch or German equivalents, and to work successfully it required veteran officers and NCOs and a cadre of veteran soldiers. The Royalist infantry was only recently raised and had few veterans; the practical effect was that while they could be drawn up in the Swedish style this was simply a façade, since they lacked the experience to use it to advantage.

There is no surviving battle plan for the Parliament army at Edgehill, but contemporary accounts show that its infantry were drawn up in two lines of battalions – as Ormonde's army had been in Ireland earlier that year – with each regiment forming either one or two battalions. The depth for the Parliament army followed an English variation on the Dutch model current since the mid-1630s, with infantry drawn up eight deep rather than the Dutch ten, and the cavalry fighting six deep. The deployment of the Parliament cavalry on its left wing included both commanded musketeer *plottons* of about 50 men each, drawn up six deep, and light artillery in the model originated by the Swedes and now forming part of the composite German style. Of the two armies, that of Parliament thus had the more modern deployment formation.

On the day, Prince Rupert chose to make an aggressive attack intended to sweep everything before him, while his Parliament opponents stood to receive his attack. The Royalist cavalry swept away the cavalry on the Parliament left wing and pursued them off the field, and at this sight one of the three Parliamentary infantry brigades broke up. However, the surviving Parliament cavalry remained on the battlefield, and the Parliament infantry and cavalry acting together had the advantage over Royalist infantry which the impetuosity of Rupert's cavalry had left without support.

Marston Moor, Donnington and Naseby, 1644–45

After 1642 the Royalists made no further use of the Swedish tactical style. Prince Rupert's campaign plans for 1643 and the early part of his 1644 campaign in the North have not survived, but Gomme's papers include redrawn copies of three other battle plans drawn up by his patron the prince. Together these form a unique insight into the development of the tactical ideas of this Royalist commander, and the European influences which shaped them. The three plans are for the deployment of Royalist armies at the battle of Marston Moor on 2 July 1644; for the army drawn up to offer battle in October the same year while recovering the artillery it had left at Donnington Castle after the second battle of Newbury (though on that occasion the Parliament army refused battle); and for the battle of Naseby on 14 June 1645.

The Royalist battle plan for Marston Moor (see page 60, '1') shows changes in Prince Rupert's tactical approach, which was now much more German in style. The infantry are drawn up in three lines, with cavalry squadrons placed

Prince Rupert's last battle plans for the Royalist army, as recorded by Sir Bernard de Gomme.
(1) The plan prepared for the relief of Donnington Castle, 9 November 1644; the action never took place, due to the failure of the Parliamentary commanders to agree to fight.
(2) The very similar plan employed by Prince Rupert at the decisive battle of Naseby, 14 June 1645 – which he lost.

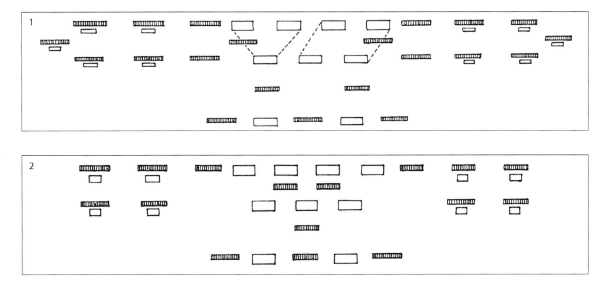

in support behind the second infantry line and a cavalry reserve behind the third or reserve infantry line. The intervals between the infantry lines follow the originally Dutch model, with the distance between the second and third lines being twice that between the first and second, leaving the third line as a final reserve. The cavalry on the wings are deployed in two lines in a chequerboard pattern, with musketeer *plottons* in support of the cavalry in the first line, and in each case a flanking regiment has been deployed to the far side of and slightly behind the first line. The Royalist deployment also shows that some of the cavalry squadrons were smaller than usual, recalling the contemporary debate as to whether large squadrons or a higher number of smaller squadrons represented the optimum deployment.

Prince Rupert's tactical ideas developed further after his defeat at Marston Moor, and his final battle plan, used for deployment at Donnington Castle and for battle at Naseby, shows further variations on the German style (see page 61). The infantry are drawn up in three lines with cavalry support, and the reserve is composed of alternating cavalry and infantry in a style very similar to that used successfully by the Duc d'Enghien at Rocroi in 1643 (see Plate F). In both the Donnington Castle and Naseby examples, Prince Rupert had infantry units from each of his brigades split between both his first and second lines, with separate units in his reserve. The cavalry squadrons are now deployed directly behind one another in a style used by some German Imperialist officers, rather than in chequerboard fashion (see Plates G & H).

The only surviving plans for the Parliament armies are for Marston Moor and Naseby. Marston Moor is not typical, as three armies were combined – the two Parliament armies of the Eastern Association and the Northern Association and an allied Scottish army. The Parliamentary and Scottish deployment at Marston Moor showed the influence of Scottish generals who had served in the Thirty Years' War. The best surviving plan is a sketch drawn by the Scottish MajGen James Lumsden; this shows the combined army with three infantry

Battle of Naseby, 14 June 1645: the copy of Robert Streeter's plan that was printed in John Rushworth's *Historical Collections*. Streeter's original plan was published with Joshua Sprigge's *Anglia Rediviva* ('England's Recovery') in London in 1647. The reduction of space between the units may be artistic licence – see Plate G. This is the view from behind Fairfax's New Model Army; see Plate G for the opposite viewpoint from behind Rupert's line.

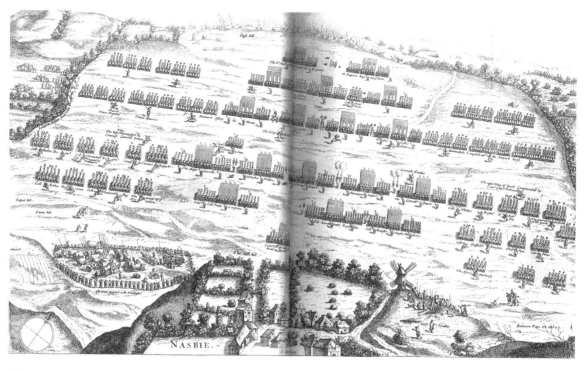

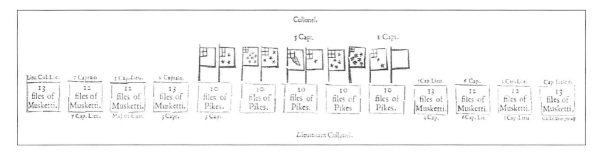

The following is a diagram with the following labels:

Collonel.

5 Capt.   1 Capt.

Lieu.Col.Lie.	7 Captain	5 Cap.Lieu.	2 Captain.						1 Cap Lieu	6 Cap.	3 Cap.Lie.	Cap Lieute.
13 files of Musketti.	12 files of Musketti.	12 files of Musketti.	13 files of Musketti.	10 files of Pikes.	10 files of Pikes.	10 files of Pikes	10 files of Pikes	10 files of Pikes.	13 files of Musketti.	12 files of Musketti.	12 files of Musketti.	13 files of Musketti,
	7 Cap. Lieu.	Major Lieu.	5 Capt.	3 Capt.					4 Cap.	6Cap.Lie.	1 Cap.Lieu	Ca.Li.Dingtrup

Lieutnant Collonel.

lines, and an unusually strong cavalry formation. This latter has three lines, each of them – and not only the first – supported with sub-units of commanded musketeers (see page 60, '3'). The infantry are formed into tactical brigades each comprising several regiments. This German practice was described by Sir James Turner, whose examples of deployments in his book *Pallas Armata* show infantry in two lines with complete brigades in each line. The deployment of the Parliament's New Model Army at Naseby is simpler than the opposing Royalist formation, having no musketeer support for its cavalry wings or cavalry support for its infantry.

The impact of civil war changed tactical thinking in England very rapidly, from the Dutch style that was conventional at the beginning of the war to the latest German composite style born of the Thirty Years' War.

The last word

For a commander in the 17th century, battle was the riskiest activity of his campaign and his career, offering opportunities for both overwhelming success and absolute disaster. He trained and prepared his troops accordingly, and deployed his army on the battlefield according to the tactical style that he preferred. In terms of which came first – the general's battle plan or the ground he would fight over – the answer in this period is the battle plan. Typically, the preferred deployment was thought through at the outset of the campaign, and then amended to suit changing strengths in his army and the nature of the ground he encountered.

Contemporary evidence for any battle in this period is fragmentary, whether from surviving accounts, from records of pay, muster or supply, or from battlefield archaeology. Essentially, we have pieces of a puzzle but will never have all of them. One advantage in understanding battlefield tactics from the contemporary commander's perspective is that it is possible to understand what he intended to do on the battlefield and what he had trained his men to do, and to use this to expand our interpretation of other records and evidence.

New Model Army infantry: deployment of Col Thomas Rainsborough's regiment for its march through the City of London on 7 August 1647, from Richard Elton's *The Compleat Body of the Art Military*. The five blocks each displaying two of the ten company colours are each annotated '10 files of Pikes', and the eight flanking blocks alternate between '13' and '12 files of Musketti', giving a ratio of two musketeers to each pikeman. The original accompanying caption reads: 'This Regiment being thus drawn up they stand in the length of their Front or Battalia, 150 abrest, and six in their depth, having two thirds of Musketiers, and one of Pikes, their number amounting in all to 900 men, each particular company consisting of 15 files, and containing in each of them 90 men apiece, but the Field-Officers Companies are many times larger.' Again, we must remember that the blocks shown in the plan are not 'companies', which were administrative entities that were divided to form the tactical blocks of pike and shot.

INDEX

References to illustrations are shown in **bold**.